W9-BKN-411

Step into...
The Stone Age

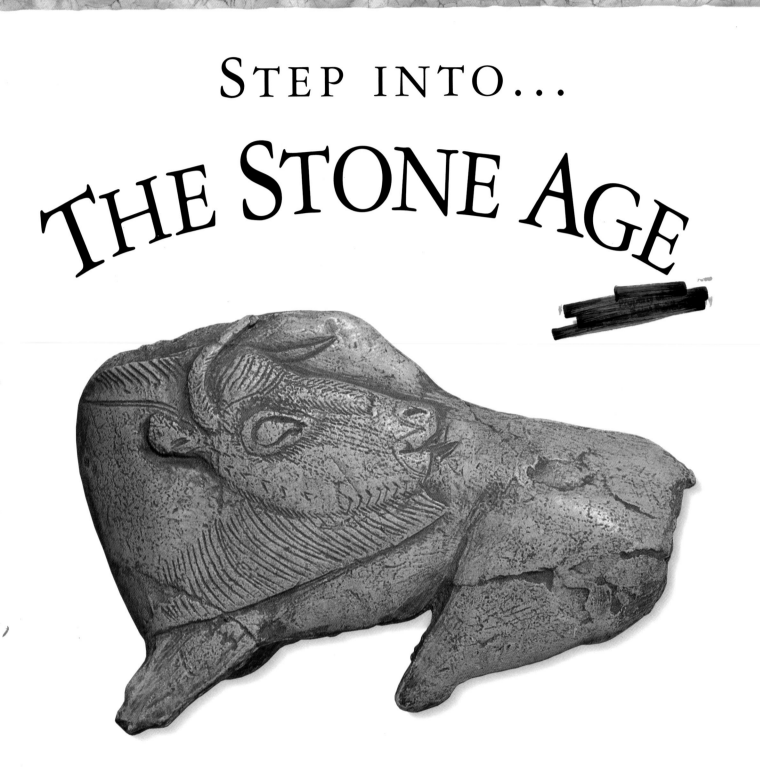

Charlotte Hurdman

Consultant: Dr Robin Holgate, Luton Museum

LORENZ BOOKS

First published in 1998 by Lorenz Books
27 West 20th Street, New York, NY 10011
LORENZ BOOKS are available for bulk purchase for
sales promotion and for premium use.
For details, write or call the sales director,
Lorenz Books, 27 West 20th Street,
New York, NY 10011; (800) 354-9657.

© Anness Publishing Limited 1998

Lorenz Books is an imprint of Anness Publishing Inc.

All rights reserved. No part of this publication may be
reproduced, stored in a retrieval system, or transmitted
in any way or by any means, electronic, mechanical,
photocopying, recording or otherwise, without the prior
written permission of the copyright holder.

ISBN 1 85967 684 7

Publisher: Joanna Lorenz
Managing Editor, Children's Books: Sue Grabham
Senior Editor: Nicole Pearson
Designer: Caroline Reeves
Illustration: Stuart Carter and Julian Baker
Photography: John Freeman
Stylist: Thomasina Smith

Anness Publishing would like to thank the following
children for modelling for this book: Mohammed Asfar,
Leon R. Banton, Afsana Begum, Ha Chu, Paula Dent,
Frankie Timothy Junior Elliot, Rikky Charles Healey,
Eva Rivera/Razbadavskite, Simon Thexton, Shereen
Thomas and Ha Vinh.

PICTURE CREDITS

b=bottom, t=top, c=center, l=left, r=right

B and C Alexander: 10tl, 12t, 27bl, 38l, 39tl, 39tr, 41t, 45br,
47tl, 60r; The Ancient Art and Architecture Collection Ltd:
pages 5tl, 11t, 35tr, 37tl, 42l, 43b, 49tr, 58r, 59tl; Heather
Angel: 25 bc; The Bridgeman Art Library: 4l, 14b, 15tr, 15br,
16l, 24l, 41c, 51br, 58l, 59cr, 61bl; The British Museum: 12c,
29tr; Peter Clayton: 35cr, 49tl, 49tr, 50bl, 51tl, 51cl; Bruce
Coleman: 25t, 28br, 35bl, 40t, 60l; Colorific 61t; Sylvia
Corday: 15tl, 22cr; C M Dixon: 5tr, 8l, 14l, 17tl, 18l, 20r, 23tl,
24r, 26t, 26b, 28t, 29tl, 30b, 33tr, 33c, 34t, 34bl, 34br, 36l,
36r, 37tr, 38r, 40cr, 42r, 44bl, 46l, 48l, 48r, 50t, 50br, 53cr,
54r, 56t, 56b, 57bl, 57br; Ecoscene: 44t, 31tr; E T Archive: 9t,
59tr; Mary Evans Picture Library: 10b, 13tl, 17tr, 27br, 35bl;
FLPA: 11cl, 29br, 51cr; Werner Forman Archive: 39bc, 47c,
54l; Fortean Picture Library: 45t, 46r, 52c; Robert Harding 5cl,
11b, 13b, 15bl, 23cl, 31tl, 31br, 53tl, 53tr; Museum of
London 28bl; Museum of Sweden: 25c

Printed and bound in Singapore.

10 9 8 7 6 5 4 3 2 1

CONTENTS

The Dawn of Humankind............. 4

The Stone Age World.... 6

People From the Past........... 8

Climate and Survival............ 10

Migration and Nomads........ 12

Social Structure...................... 14

Communication and Counting..... 16

Shelter.............................. 18

Fire and Light............................ 20

Food for Gathering...................... 22

Fish and Shells........................ 24

Hunting Animals................................. 26

The First Crops................................. 28

Taming Animals............... 30

Stone Technology........ 32

Carving Wood and Bone................ 34

Crafts.................................. 36

Clothing.............................. 38

Ornament and Decoration........... 40

The Arts.............................. 42

Trade and Distribution............. 44

Transport on Land and Sea............. 46

Warfare and Weapons........................ 48

Religion and Magic........................ 50

Monuments of Wood and Stone........................ 52

Journey through Life........................ 54

Neolithic Villages........................ 56

The End of an Era........................ 58

The Stone Age Today................ 60

Glossary........................ 62

Index................64

The Dawn of Humankind

THE FIRST PERIOD in human history is called the Stone Age. Stone was used to make tools and other objects. Some of these objects survive today. Wood, bone and plant fibers were also used, but they rotted, leaving little trace.

Our earliest human ancestors were making tools from stone at least two million years ago, but our story really starts with the arrival of modern humans, called *Homo sapiens sapiens,* about 100,000 years ago. The Stone Age is part of human prehistory, which means that it took place before there were any written records. Archaeologists have to be detectives, piecing together what might have happened. Special techniques, such as radiocarbon dating, help experts to figure out what life was like thousands of years ago. We can also look at modern-day hunter-gatherer cultures for clues as to how Stone Age people lived.

SKELETONS AND BURIALS
This is the skeleton of a Neanderthal man who was buried about 60,000 years ago. Human remains and the objects buried with them can tell experts a lot about early people.

CAVE PAINTINGS
This beautiful painting of a bison is from the caves at Altamira in Spain. It was painted in about 13,000 B.C. by prehistoric hunters. Cave paintings often show animals that were hunted at the time.

TIMELINE 120,000–10,000 B.C.

The huge periods over which human prehistory has taken place mean that even with scientific dating, timings can only be approximate.

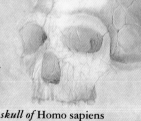

120,000 B.C. Neanderthal people, or *Homo sapiens neanderthalensis*, are living in Europe and western Asia. There is evidence in Iraq that they are burying their dead.

Neanderthal woman

100,000 B.C. Modern humans, or *Homo sapiens sapiens,* are living in eastern and southern Africa

skull of Homo sapiens neanderthalensis

skull of Homo sapiens sapiens

50,000 B.C. Humans settle in Australia from southeastern Asia.

42,000 B.C. Red ocher earth is mined in Swaziland in Africa.

38,000 B.C. Modern humans are living at Cro-Magnon in France.

| 120,000 B.C. | 100,000 B.C. | 80,000 B.C. | 60,000 B.C. | 30,000 B.C |

SCULPTURES

Small carvings of prehistoric women are called Venus figurines. This one was made around 23,000 B.C. The many sculptures that have been found can give clues to Stone Age people's ideas and beliefs.

SCENES FROM LIFE

This rock engraving, or carving, from Namibia shows two giraffes. It was carved by hunters in southern Africa around 6000 B.C. The North American continent is the only one where early prehistoric art like this has not yet been found.

TOOLS

Looking at stone tools can tell us how they may have been made and used. Tools such as this hand-axe and these scrapers were used for preparing meat and hides.

CLUES IN CAVES

Many rock shelters and natural caves, like this one in Malta, have been lived in for thousands of years. Much of our knowledge about prehistoric people has been found by carefully digging through layers of rock and soil in sites like this. Many rock homes seem to have been lived in for thousands of years before being abandoned.

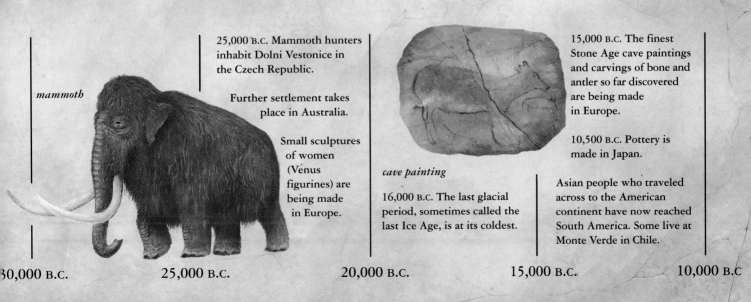

mammoth

25,000 B.C. Mammoth hunters inhabit Dolni Vestonice in the Czech Republic.

Further settlement takes place in Australia.

Small sculptures of women (Venus figurines) are being made in Europe.

cave painting

16,000 B.C. The last glacial period, sometimes called the last Ice Age, is at its coldest.

15,000 B.C. The finest Stone Age cave paintings and carvings of bone and antler so far discovered are being made in Europe.

10,500 B.C. Pottery is made in Japan.

Asian people who traveled across to the American continent have now reached South America. Some live at Monte Verde in Chile.

30,000 B.C.   25,000 B.C.   20,000 B.C.   15,000 B.C.   10,000 B.C

The Stone Age World

THE STONE AGE is the longest period of human history. It covers such a vast time period that it is often divided into stages, according to the type of tools people were using. The first and by far the longest stage was the Palaeolithic period, or Old Stone Age, which began more than two million years ago. During this time, people made the first stone tools. It was followed by the Mesolithic period, or Middle Stone Age, around 10,000 B.C. During this period people began to use new tools, such as bows and arrows, to hunt deer and wild pigs. From about 8000 B.C., the Neolithic period, or New Stone Age, began with the start of farming. However, the Stone Age has lasted for different periods of time in different parts of the world, so these distinctions are not always helpful. The Stone Age came to an end when people began to work metals on a large scale.

Modern human beings now live all over the earth, but views vary about how this happened. Some experts think we evolved, or developed, in Africa before spreading out into Asia and Europe. Others think we evolved separately in different parts of the world. The first people to reach America probably crossed from Siberia in Russia when the Bering Strait was dry land. This may have been around 13,000 B.C. or even earlier. By about 10,000 B.C., however, people had reached right to the tip of South America.

mastodon, Canada
20,000BC

bisons,
North America
9000BC

NORTH AMERICA

CENTRAL AMERICA

agriculture, South America
7000BC

Origins of agriculture

cave art, Argentina
8500BC

TIMELINE 10,000 B.C.–5000 B.C.

10,000 B.C. The last glacial period ends and the climate becomes warmer.

By this date, humans have reached Patagonia at the tip of South America.

Grindstones for making flour are used in Egypt and Nubia in northern Africa.

Mammoths and woolly rhinoceroses are now extinct in central and western Europe.

einkorn wheat

9000 B.C. The Clovis culture is flourishing in North America.

Einkorn wheat is harvested in Syria.

Many large mammals have become extinct in America.

8500 B.C. Sheep and goats are now domesticated in Mesopotamia (modern Iraq).

Squash, peppers and beans are being grown in Peru.

Squash, peppers and beans

8000 B.C. Grains are cultivated in the Near East.

A lasting settlement is built at Jericho in Jordan and begins to grow to become the first town.

Mesolithic tools

10,000 B.C.   9000 B.C.   8000 B.C.   7000 B.C.

Property of
Bayport-Blue Point Public Library

EUROPE

migrating reindeer, Russia
15,000BC

*clay figurine,
Czech Republic*
24,000BC

ASIA

cave art, France
15,000BC

*settlement,
Turkey*
6,500BC

pottery, Japan
10,500BC

*rock art,
Sahara*
6000BC

Peking Man, China
460,0000BC

AFRICA

Homo erectus *skull,
Java,* 120,000BC

Homo habilis *skull, Kenya
2.5 million years ago*

SOUTH AMERICA

N

cave art, Namibia
8000BC

AUSTRALIA

*indigenous peoples,
Australia*
50,000BC

THE STONE AGE WORLD
This map shows places of
importance during the Stone Age.

7000 B.C. Pottery is made in China and the Near East.

The town of Çatal Hüyük in Turkey is established.

The Bering Strait separates North America from Asia.

6300 B.C. Potatoes are cultivated in Peru.

Dugout canoes are used at Pesse in the Netherlands.

*dugout canoe
being paddled*

6000 B.C. Cattle herding, farming and rock art are all taking place in the Sahara.

Copper and gold are first used in Mesopotamia.

Farming begins in Greece and southeastern Europe.

Crops and sheep are introduced into Egypt from the Near East.

sheep

Britain is cut off from the continent of Europe by rising sea levels.

5500 B.C. Irrigation is practiced in Mesopotamia.

5300 B.C. Farming is taking place and pottery is made in central Europe.

7000 B.C.

6000 B.C.

5000 B.C.

People from the Past

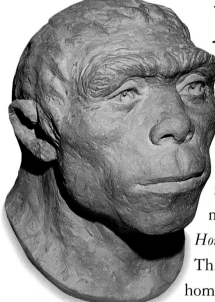

MODERN HUMANS and their most recent ancestors are called hominids. The first hominids formed two main groups—*Australopithecus* and *Homo. Australopithecus* first appeared about four million years ago and died out about one million years ago. *Homo habilis* appeared about two and a half million years ago and, like *Australopithecus,* lived in southern and eastern Africa.

About two million years ago, a new kind of hominid, *Homo erectus,* appeared. This was the first hominid to leave Africa, moving into Asia and later Europe. Eventually, *Homo erectus* evolved, or developed, into *Homo sapiens,* which evolved into *Homo sapiens sapiens,* or modern humans. By 10,000 B.C. *Homo sapiens sapiens* had settled on every continent except Antarctica.

PEKING MAN
This reconstruction is of a type of *Homo erectus* whose remains were found in China. These early people lived from about 460,000 to 230,000 years ago. Experts believe they may have been the first people to make regular use of fire.

CRO-MAGNON PEOPLE
The burial of a young Cro-Magnon man, whose remains were found in a Welsh cave, is shown in this picture. The body was sprinkled with red ochre and wore bracelets and a necklace of animal teeth. The Cro-Magnons were the first modern people to live in Europe, about 40,000 years ago.

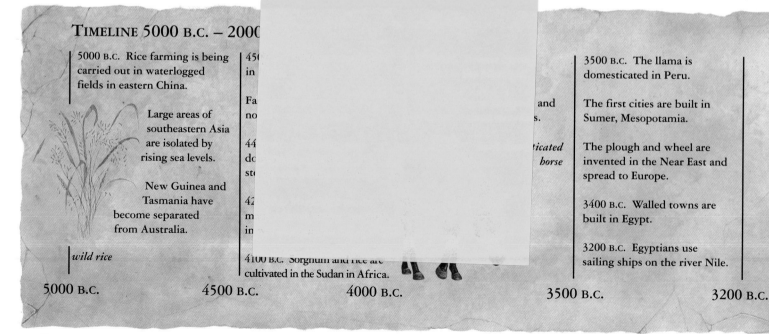

TIMELINE 5000 B.C. – 200

5000 B.C. Rice farming is being carried out in waterlogged fields in eastern China.

Large areas of southeastern Asia are isolated by rising sea levels.

New Guinea and Tasmania have become separated from Australia.

wild rice

45[...] in [...]

Fa[...] no[...]

44[...] d[...] st[...]

42[...] m[...] in [...]

4100 B.C. Sorghum and rice are cultivated in the Sudan in Africa.

[...] and [...]s.

[...]ticated *horse*

3500 B.C. The llama is domesticated in Peru.

The first cities are built in Sumer, Mesopotamia.

The plough and wheel are invented in the Near East and spread to Europe.

3400 B.C. Walled towns are built in Egypt.

3200 B.C. Egyptians use sailing ships on the river Nile.

5000 B.C.   4500 B.C.   4000 B.C.   3500 B.C.   3200 B.C.

AUSTRALOPITHECUS
4.5 to 2 million years ago

Archaeologists believe that our earliest ancestors came from Africa. One group, Australopithecus Africanus, walked upright.

HOMO HABILIS
2 to 1.6 million years ago

Homo habilis *walked upright but had long arms. Habilis was probably the first hominid to make stone tools and to hunt.*

HOMO ERECTUS
1.6 million to 400,000 years ago

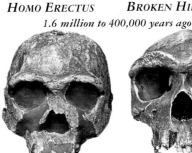

This hominid had a bigger brain than Habilis *and may have been as tall and heavy as modern people. Erecutus was a skillful hunter. Erectus invented new kinds of tools, used fire, lived in rock shelters and built huts.*

BROKEN HILL MAN
1.6 million to 400,000 years ago

This hominid was another Homo erectus. *Erectus invented new kinds of tools, used fire, lived in rock shelters and built huts.*

NEANDERTHAL MAN
120,000 to 33,000 years ago

Homo sapiens neanderthalis (Neanderthals) made flint tools. Neanderthals are thought to have been the first people to bury their dead.

MODERN MAN
100,000 years ago

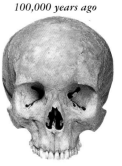

Our own subspecies, Homo sapiens sapiens *(modern man), developed over 100,000 years ago.*

NEANDERTHAL PEOPLE

The Neanderthals were a subspecies of *Homo sapiens* who flourished in Europe and western Asia from about 120,000 to 33,000 years ago, during the last glacial, or cold, period. They had larger brains than modern humans, with sloping foreheads and heavy brows.

HOMO SAPIENS

This skull belonged to an early human being. The species *Homo sapiens* may have evolved about 400,000 years ago.

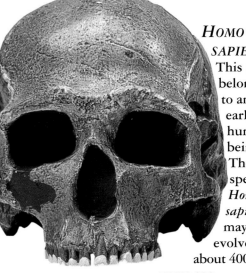

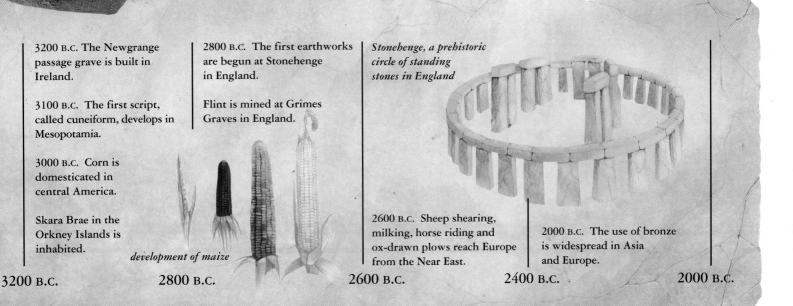

3200 B.C. The Newgrange passage grave is built in Ireland.

3100 B.C. The first script, called cuneiform, develops in Mesopotamia.

3000 B.C. Corn is domesticated in central America.

Skara Brae in the Orkney Islands is inhabited.

development of maize

2800 B.C. The first earthworks are begun at Stonehenge in England.

Flint is mined at Grimes Graves in England.

Stonehenge, a prehistoric circle of standing stones in England

2600 B.C. Sheep shearing, milking, horse riding and ox-drawn plows reach Europe from the Near East.

2000 B.C. The use of bronze is widespread in Asia and Europe.

3200 B.C.   2800 B.C.   2600 B.C.   2400 B.C.   2000 B.C.

Climate and Survival

COVERED BY ICE
Ancient ice still forms this Alaskan glacier. The height of the last glacial period was reached about 18,000 years ago. At this time, almost 30 percent of the earth was covered by ice, including large parts of North America, Europe and Asia, as well as New Zealand and southern Argentina. Temperatures dropped, and sea levels fell by over 100 yards.

ONE CHANGING ASPECT of our earth affected Stone Age people more than anything else—the climate. Over many thousands of years, the climate gradually grew cooler and then just as slowly warmed up again. This cycle happened many times, changing the landscape and the plants and animals that lived in it.

During cool periods, called glacials, sea levels dropped, exposing more land. Herds of animals grazed vast grasslands and the cold, bare tundra farther north. When temperatures rose, so did sealevels, isolating people on newly formed islands. Woodlands gradually covered the plains.

DEER HUNTER
In warmer periods, forest animals like this red deer replaced bison, mammoths and reindeer, which moved north. Humans followed the grazing herds or began to hunt forest game.

ANIMALS OF THE COLD
Mammoths were the largest mammals adapted to a colder climate, grazing the northern plains. The related mastodon was found in North America. Reindeer, horses, musk oxen, woolly rhinoceroses and bison were common, too.

Animal Extinctions

This painting of a mammoth is from a cave in southwestern France. By 10,000 B.C., mammoths and woolly rhinoceroses were extinct in central and western Europe, as were bison and reindeer. In North America, mammoths, mastodons, camelids and many other large animal species vanished abruptly by 9000 B.C. Even in tropical Africa, the rich variety of animals of the savanna was reduced at the end of the last glacial period.

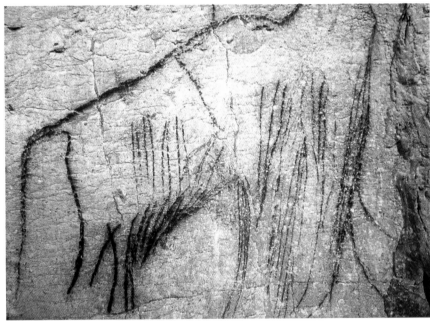

Wild Boar

Pigs, such as wild boar, are adapted to living in a forest habitat. They use their snouts and feet to root for food on the forest floor. Pigs were one of the first animals to be domesticated because they will eat almost anything.

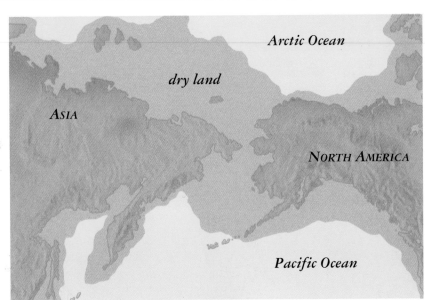

Arctic Ocean

dry land

Asia

North America

Pacific Ocean

Isolated Islands

The White Cliffs of Dover are a famous landmark on England's southeastern coast, but this was not always so. During the last glacial period, Ireland, Great Britain and France were linked. When the ice began to melt, areas of low-lying land were gradually flooded, causing Britain to became an island by 6000 B.C.

Land Bridges

This illustration shows how two continents were joined by tundra during the last glacial period. Early man could migrate across the dry land that had been created over the Bering Straits and cross from Asia to North America. When the ice melted, the crossing was no longer possible and the continents were once again separated by sea. There were many land bridges during the glacial periods, including one that connected Great Britain to continental Europe.

Migration and Nomads

THE FIRST HUMANS did not lead a settled life, living in the same place all the time. Instead, they were nomads, moving around throughout the year. They did this in order to find food. Early people did not grow crops or keep animals. They hunted wild animals and collected berries, nuts and other plants. This is called a hunter-gatherer way of life. Moving from one place to another is called migration. Some Stone Age migrations were seasonal, following the herds of game. Others were caused by natural disasters, such as forest fires or volcanic eruptions. Changes in the climate and rising populations also forced people to move in search of new territory. After humans learned how to farm, many settled down in permanent homes to raise their crops.

MIGRATING HERDS
A huge herd of reindeer begins its spring migration across northern Norway. The Sami, or Lapp people, have lived in the Arctic regions of Sweden and Norway since ancient times. They herd reindeer for their meat and milk, following the herds north in the spring and camping in tents called *lavos*.

ANTLER HARPOON
This antler harpoon was found at Star Carr, in North Yorkshire, England. Antlers were easily carved into barbed points to make harpoons. The points were tied to spears and used for fishing and hunting.

SEASONAL CAMPS
In mesolithic times, the hunter-gatherers moved camp at different times of year. In late spring and summer, inland and coastal camps were used. Red and roe deer were hunted in the woods. Fish, shellfish, seals and wild birds were caught or gathered. Meat, hides and antlers were cut up and prepared, then taken to a more sheltered winter settlement.

hunting camp

hunting camp

hunting camp

hunting camp

winter base camp

coastal fishing camp

The changing climate caused changes in vegetation. Heather, mosses and lichens grew on the cold tundra that covered much of the land during glacial periods. On the edge of the tundra were forests of pine, larch and spruce. As the climate warmed, the first trees to colonize open areas were silver birches. Gradually, the birches were replaced by oaks, hazels and elms. As forests grew larger, people found there was enough food to hunt and gather in one area without the need to migrate.

moss   *pine*

NATIVE AMERICANS

The Plains Indians of North America were nomads, living in cone-shaped buffalo-hide tents called tepees. Native Americans of the eastern plains, such as the Dakota shown above, lived mainly in permanent settlements, using their tepees for summer and autumn hunts. In the 1800s, the Plains Indians were forced by the United States government to live on reservations. They took their tepees with them and tried to preserve part of their traditional way of life.

NOMADS IN THE DESERT

Although their numbers are dwindling, the Bedouin still live as nomadic herders in the dry regions of the Near East and Africa. They keep camels, sheep and goats to provide milk and meat. Their animals are also sold for other foods, such as flour, dates and coffee. Bedouins live in tents made from woven goat hair. They move from place to place in search of grazing land for their animals, just as people have done for thousands of years.

Social Structure

I̶N STONE AGE TIMES, there were very few people in the world. Experts estimate that the world's population in 13,000 B.C. was only about eight million. Today it is nearer six billion (six thousand million). We can make guesses about how Stone Age people lived together by looking at hunter-gatherer societies of today.

Although people lived in families as we do, these families lived together in groups called clans. All the members of a clan were related to each other, usually through their mother's family or by marriage. Clans were large enough to protect and feed everyone, but not so large that they were unmanageable. All the members of a clan, including children, were involved in finding and gathering food for everyone. Clans were probably also part of larger tribes, which may have met up at certain times of year, such as for the summer hunt. The members of a tribe shared a language and a way of life. When people learned how to farm, populations increased and societies began to be organized in more complicated ways.

MOTHER GODDESSES
This baked-clay sculpture from Turkey was made around 6000 B.C. She may have been worshipped as a goddess of motherhood. Families were often traced through the female line because mothers give birth, while fathers may remain unknown.

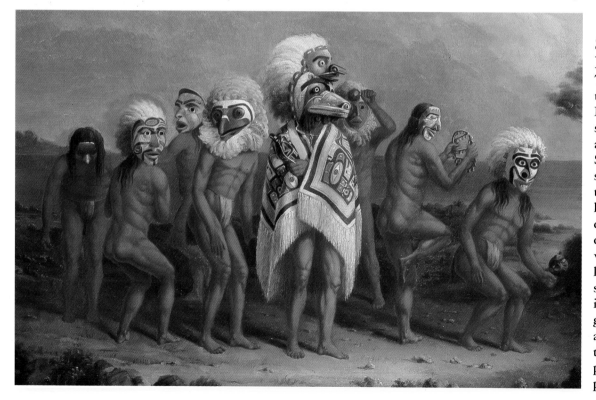

SHAMAN LEADERS
This painting from the 1800s shows Native American shamans performing a ritual dance. Shamans were the spiritual leaders of their tribes. They knew the dances, chants, prayers and ceremonies that would bring good luck and please the spirits. Shamanism is found in hunter-gatherer societies around the world today and was practiced in prehistoric times.

TRIBAL CHIEF

This man is a Zulu chief from South Africa. His higher rank is shown by what he wears. In prehistoric times, tribes might have been ruled by chiefs or councils of elders. An old man buried at Sungir in Russia around 23,000 B.C. was probably a chief. His body was found richly decorated with fox teeth and beads made of mammoth ivory.

SCENES FROM LONG AGO

Paintings on cliff walls in the Sahara Desert show hippopotamuses being hunted and herders tending cattle. Other images show a woman pounding flour, as well as wedding ceremonies and a family with a dog. They show that in 6000 B.C., the Sahara was a fertile area with organized communities.

A CYCLADIC FIGURINE

Between 3000 and 2000 B.C., some of the finest prehistoric sculpture was made on the Greek islands known as the Cyclades. This figurine is made of ground marble and shows a slender woman with her arms folded above her waist. Figurines showing musicians with harps and flutes have also been found. Such sculptures come from complex societies.

A TRADITIONAL WAY OF LIFE

The man on the left is helping a boy prepare for his coming-of-age ceremony in Papua New Guinea. Traditional ways of life are still strong in that country, where there are many remote tribes. In some villages, all the men live together, rather than with their wives and children. This allows them to organize their work, such as hunting, more easily.

Communication and Counting

OUR EARLY HUMAN ANCESTORS were communicating with each other using words and gestures as long ago as 300,000 B.C. Eventually, complex languages began to develop to pass on skills and knowledge. Hunters may have used a special sign language when tracking game, leaving markers to signal the route and imitating animal and bird sounds.

From about 37,000 B.C., people began to carve marks on bones and to use pebbles as simple counting devices. Days may have been counted on calendar sticks. In some cave paintings, experts have noticed dots and symbols that may be counting tallies or the beginnings of a writing system.

By about 7000 B.C., tokens with symbols to represent numbers and objects were being used by traders in the Near East. They may have led to the first written script. This developed about 3100 B.C. and was a kind of picture-writing called cuneiform.

TALLY STICK
Notches carved on wooden sticks, or in this case on the leg bone of a baboon, may have been used as counting devices or as simple calendars. This one dates from about 35,000 B.C. Similar sticks are used by some groups of people living in southern Africa today.

PICTURES AND SYMBOLS
This cave painting of a wild horse comes from Lascaux in southwestern France. It was painted in about 15,000 B.C. The horse is surrounded by symbols that, along with dots and notches, may have been a way of keeping track of migrating animals.

HAND ART
You will need: self-drying clay, rolling pin and board, modeling tool, sandpaper, yellow and red acrylic paints, water, two spray bottles.

1 Roll out the clay, giving it a lumpy surface like a cave wall. Trim the edges with a modeling tool to make a stone tablet.

2 Leave the clay to dry. When it is hard, rub the tablet with sandpaper to get rid of sharp edges and make a smooth surface.

3 Mix the paint with water and fill the spray bottles. Put one hand on the tablet and spray plenty of yellow paint around it.

WRITING DEVELOPMENT

This Sumerian clay tablet was made around 3100 B.C. It uses characters based on picture symbols to give an account of a year's harvest. As cuneiform writing developed, people wanted to express abstract ideas, such as good or bad, so they changed symbols already in use, often by adding marks.

SMOKE SIGNALS

This engraving from the late 1800s shows Native Americans using smoke signals to communicate with each other. Human beings have spent most of their history without written language, but this does not mean they were always unable to communicate or record important information.

HANDS ON

These hand stencils are from a cave in Argentina. They are similar to those found on rock walls in Europe, Africa and Australia. They may have been a way for prehistoric artists to sign their work.

4 Keeping your hand in exactly the same place, spray on the red paint so that you are left with a clear, sharp outline.

5 When you have finished spraying, remove your hand. Be careful not to smudge the paint, and leave the tablet to dry.

The artist of the original Argentine hand-painting sprayed paint around his or her hand. This was done either by blowing through a reed, or by spitting paint onto the cave wall!

Shelter

PEOPLE HAVE always needed protection from the weather. During most of the last 100,000 years, the earth's climate was much colder than it is today. People lived in huts in the open during summer, but when harsh weather came, families moved into caves. They built stone windbreaks across the entrances and put up huts inside to give further protection from the storms and cold. In summer, as they followed the herds of game, hunters built shelters of branches and leaves. Families lived in camps of huts made of branches and animal skins. Farther north, where there were no caves and few trees, people built huts from mammoths' leg bones and tusks. Wherever they settled, however, it was very important to be near a supply of fresh water.

CAVES AND ROCK SHELTERS
This is the entrance to a rock shelter in southwestern France. Neanderthal people were the first to occupy this site, in about 100,000 B.C. People usually lived close to the entrance of a cave, where the light was best and the sun's warmth could reach them.

MAMMOTH-BONE HOME
This is a reconstruction of a mammoth-hunter's house. It was built in about 13,000 B.C. in Ukraine. The gaps between the bones were filled with moss and shrubs. The entire structure was then covered with mammoth hide or turf.

A HUNTER'S HOME
You will need: self-drying clay, board, modeling tool, cardboard, brown-green acrylic paint, paintbrush, scissors, twigs, ruler, white glue, jar of water, fake grass or green fabric.

1 Roll out lengths of clay to form long and short mammoth bones and tusks. Then make some stones in different sizes.

2 Use the modeling tool to shape the ends of the bones and make the stones uneven. Leave the pieces, carefully separated, to dry.

3 Spread some modeling clay roughly over a piece of cardboard. Paint the clay a brown-green color and leave to dry.

MOBILE HOME

This model tepee was made in 1904 by the Cheyenne people of the Great Plains in the United States. Prehistoric people may have lived in tents or huts like this, made from branches covered with animal hides. They were quick to put up and take down, and could be folded for carrying. Portable homes were essential for people following migrating herds of animals.

SHELTERS OF TURF AND STONE

This is the outside of a Neolithic house in the village of Skara Brae in the Orkney Islands. It was built around 3000 B.C. The buildings were sunk into the ground and surrounded with turf to protect them from bad storms. Covered passages linked the houses.

A BURIED SITE

The village of Skara Brae in the Orkney Islands was built of stone because there were no local trees for building. Even the furniture inside was made of stone. In about 2000 B.C., the whole village was buried by a sandstorm, preserving the site until it was exposed by another great storm in 1850.

Where wood was scarce, heavy mammoth bones were used to weight down grass and animal hides covering a hunter's house.

4 Use a pair of scissors to cut the twigs so that they are 6 inches long. You will need about eight evenly sized twigs in all.

5 Push the twigs into the modeling clay to form a cone-shaped frame. Glue a few stones onto the clay at the base of the twigs.

6 Cover the twigs with pieces of fake grass or fabric glued in place. Be sure not to cover up the stones around the base.

7 Neatly glue the long mammoth bones and tusks all over the outside. Fill in gaps with smaller bones. Leave it all to dry.

Fire and Light

Our ancestor *Homo erectus* learned to use fire at least 700,000 years ago. This early human ate cooked food and had warmth and light at night. Fire was useful to keep wild animals away and to harden the tips of wooden spears. Hunters waving flaming branches could scare large animals into ambushes. *Homo erectus* probably did not know how to make fire, but found smoldering logs after natural forest fires. Campfires were carefully kept lit, and hot ashes may have been carried to each new camp. Eventually, people learned to make fire by rubbing two dry sticks together. Then they found that striking a stone against a kind of rock called pyrite made a spark. By 4000 B.C., the bow drill had been invented. This made lighting a fire much easier.

STONE LAMP
Prehistoric artists used simple stone lamps like this as they decorated the walls of caves 17,000 years ago. A lighted wick of moss, twine or fur was put in a stone bowl filled with animal fat. Wooden splinters or rushes dipped in beeswax or resin were also used.

AROUND THE HEARTH
This is the inside of a Neolithic house at Skara Brae in the Orkney Islands. In the center is a stone hearth, surrounded by beds, chairs and a dresser, also all made from stone. The smoke from the fire escaped through a hole in the turf roof. The large stones surrounding the hearth helped to protect the fire from being put out by drafts.

A MODEL BOW DRILL

You will need: thick piece of dowel, craft knife, sandpaper, wood stain, jar of water, balsa wood, brush, modeling tool, clay, rolling pin, scissors, chamois leather, raffia or straw.

1 Ask an adult to shape one end of the dowel into a point with a craft knife. The blade should always angle away from the body.

2 Lightly sand down the stick and paint it with wood stain. Ask an adult to cut out a balsa-wood base. Paint the base, too.

3 Use the modeling tool to gouge a small hole in the center of the balsa-wood base. The dowel should fit in this hole.

BUSH FIRES

Before people learned to make fire, they made use of accidental fires like this one in Africa, perhaps set off by lightning or the sun's heat. Early people learned to use fire for cooking. Many vegetable plants are poisonous when raw but harmless when cooked. Fire was also used for hunting. A line of fire was lit, and then the hunters would catch animals as they fled.

FIRE STARTER

A Kalahari bushman uses a modern bow drill to start a fire. The string of a bow is used to twist a wooden drill round and round as the bow is moved backward and forward. The drill's point rests on a wooden base. The rubbing of the drill on the base creates heat, which is used to set fire to a small heap of tinder, such as moss. The tinder is then added to a pile of dry grass and small sticks.

To hold the drill upright, prehistoric people used a stone or piece of wood at the top. Some had a wooden mouthpiece to hold the drill upright and free the other hand to hold the base.

4 Roll out the clay and cut out a bone shape. Make a hole in each end and smooth the sides with your fingers. Let it harden.

5 Use a pair of scissors to cut a thin strip of leather about twice as long as the bone. This is the thong used to twist the drill.

6 Tie the strip of leather to the bone. Thread the strip through both holes, tying a knot at each end to secure the leather.

7 Scatter straw or raffia around the base. Wrap the leather thong around the drill and place the point in the central hole.

Food for Gathering

MATTOCK

This mattock, or digging tool, was made from an antler. It dates from between 8000 B.C. and 4000 B.C. It has a hole drilled through it, in which a wooden handle would have been fitted.

STONE AGE hunter-gatherers had a very varied diet. They gradually discovered which plants they could eat and where they grew. From spring to autumn, women and children foraged for seeds, berries, nuts and roots. They found birds' eggs and the shoots and leaves of vegetable plants. In summer, plants such as peas, beans, squash and cucumbers were picked, and the seeds of wild grasses were collected. The summer sun also ripened wild dates, grapes, figs, blueberries and cranberries. In autumn, there were nuts such as almonds, pine nuts, walnuts, hazelnuts and acorns. These were stored underground; fruits and berries were dried to preserve them.

Insects, caterpillars and snails were food, too! Wild honeycomb and herbs added flavor. The foragers used digging sticks to unearth roots, while leather bags and woven baskets held food safely.

INSECT GRUB

This is a witchetty grub, the large white larva of a goat moth. These grubs are eaten as a delicacy by Australian Aborigines. Insects such as ants, grasshoppers, beetles and termites were healthy, high-protein food for Stone Age people.

BIRDS' EGGS

Prehistoric people ate many kinds of birds' eggs, from tiny quail eggs to huge ostrich eggs. These eggs were laid by a pheasant, a bird native to Asia. Eggs are rich in protein, vitamins and minerals, which make them a valuable food. Eggshells were also used to make beads for jewelry.

STEWED FRUIT

You will need: a large saucepan, 2 cups blueberries, 2 cups blackberries, 2 cups hazelnuts, wooden spoon, honeycomb, tablespoon, ladle, serving bowl.

1 Always choose firm, fresh fruit and wash it and your hands before you begin. First pour the blueberries into the pan.

2 Next pour in the blackberries. Use a wooden spoon to stir them gently into the blueberries, without crushing the fruit.

3 Shake in the whole hazelnuts and carefully stir the fruit and nuts once again until they are all thoroughly mixed.

WEAR AND TEAR
This Neanderthal skull is around 60,000 years old. From remains like this, experts can tell a lot about prehistoric people's diets. Stone Age people ate very few sweet things, so their teeth are rarely decayed, but people who ate a lot of grain often have very worn teeth from the hard outer cases of the seeds. Later, grain ground into flour contained a lot of grit, which also wore down teeth.

AUTUMN'S BOUNTY
The food that prehistoric people ate came mostly from plants. Each clan (tribe) had its own well-defined territory, over which it roamed, and each may have followed a seasonal route to visit favorite food plants. Dandelion leaves and nettle leaves could be gathered in the open countryside. Woodlands in autumn were a particularly rich source of food, with plenty of fruits and nuts. Many kinds of edible fungi, too, flourish in damp woodlands, especially during autumn.

nettle leaves

dandelion leaves   *woodland fungus*

LOOKING FOR HONEY
This Mbuti man in the Democratic Republic of the Congo is smoking out bees from their nest in order to collect the honey. Prehistoric people may also have used fire to rob bees of their store. Collecting honey was worth the danger as it is rich in energy-giving carbohydrates, and its sweetness made foods tasty.

4 Add six tablespoons of honey from the comb. Now ask an adult to put the pan on the stove and bring it slowly to a boil.

5 Simmer the fruit and nuts very gently for 20 minutes. Leave to cool. Use a ladle to transfer your dessert to a serving bowl.

Prehistoric people would have cooked fruit in a similar way to preserve it as jam. Clay pots, rather than metal saucepans, were used for cooking and storing.

Fish and Shells

Toward the end of the last glacial period, about 12,000 years ago, the world's climate began to warm up. Melting ice flooded low-lying plains and fed many lakes, marshes and rivers. Trees grew across the grasslands and tundra, and bands of hunters started to settle down in campsites, some of which were permanent, beside seashores, lakes and rivers. Fishing and gathering shellfish became increasingly important sources of food for many people. Along the seashore, people foraged for seaweed and shellfish such as mussels, whelks, clams and crabs. They also hunted many kinds of fish, seals and seabirds. Rivers and lakes were full of fish such as salmon and pike, as well as crayfish, turtles, ducks and other waterbirds. Fishing was done from boats or the shore, using hooks, harpoons and nets. Traps made of woven willow were put at one end of a dam built across a stream. As fish swam through, they were caught in the trap.

SEAL HUNTER
The traditional way of life of the Inuit is probably very similar to that of prehistoric hunter-fishers. The Inuit have lived along Arctic coasts for thousands of years.

BONE HARPOONS
These bone harpoon heads from southwestern France date from around 12,000 B.C. They would have had wooden shafts and been attached to strips of leather or sinew.

A MODEL HARPOON
You will need: dowel, craft knife, wood stain, self-drying clay, wooden board, ruler, pencil, white cardboard, scissors, modeling tool, white glue, paintbrush, paint, jar of water, leather laces or strong string.

1 Ask an adult to cut down one end of a long thick dowel, using a craft knife. Cuts should be made away from the body.

2 Paint the dowel with wood stain and leave it to dry. The stain will darken the wood to make it look older and stronger.

3 Roll out a piece of white clay to make a shaft about 6 inches long. Shape one end of the clay to a rounded point.

FOOD FROM THE SEASHORE

The seashore provided a plentiful source of food all year round. Mussels, cockles, whelks, oysters, scallops, periwinkles, razors clams, crabs and lobsters could be found along sandy beaches and in rock pools. Seaweed and the fleshy leaves of rock samphire were also collected from rocks and cliffs.

edible crab

mussel   *rock samphire*

FEARSOME FIGHTER

The pike lives in lakes and rivers. It is a powerful fish and a terrifying predator. Prehistoric people fished for pike from dugout canoes in late spring and early summer.

FISHING TACKLE

Fish hooks, made from carved bone, wood, antler, flint or shell, were attached to a strong line. A caught fish was stunned with a club before being hauled into the canoe.

Prehistoric hunters used harpoons for catching fish and for hunting reindeer and bison.

A SHELLFISH MIDDEN

These are the remains of a pile of triton shells found in Australia. Heaps of discarded shells and fish and animal bones are called middens. Archaeologists can learn a lot from middens. Besides giving clues as to what people ate, the shells often contain broken tools, thrown out with the rest of the rubbish.

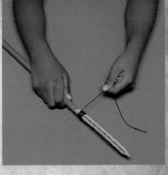

4 Draw out a serrated edge for a row of barbs on a strip of cardboard about 1 inch by 4 inches. Carefully cut out the barbs.

5 Use a modeling tool to make a slot down one side of the clay harpoon. Leave the clay to dry, then glue the barbs into the slot.

6 When the glue has dried, paint the head of the harpoon a suitable stone color, such as grayish brown.

7 Using a leather lace or strong string, tightly bind the harpoon head to the cut-down end of the wooden shaft.

Hunting Animals

DURING THE LAST GLACIAL PERIOD, clans hunted great herds of bison, horses, reindeer and mammoths that roamed the tundra and grasslands. At first they used stone axes and wooden spears. Later, spears with bone or flint barbs were developed, and spear-throwers were used to propel the spears farther and harder. Animals were attacked directly or caught in pitfall traps and snares. An entire herd might be chased over a cliff or into an ambush— this was a good way to build up a large supply of meat. As forests spread over the land, forest animals were hunted with bows and arrows. By about 12,000 B.C., hunters were using tame dogs to help in the chase. Every part of a kill was used. The meat was cooked for food or dried to preserve it. Hides were made into clothes, and animal fat was used in lamps. Bones and antlers were made into tools and weapons.

ANIMAL CARVINGS
This figure of a bison licking its back was carved from a reindeer's antler in about 12,000 B.C. It may have been part of a spear-thrower. Hunters often decorated their weapons with carvings of the animals they hunted.

BISON CAVE PAINTING
These two bison were painted on a cave wall in France around 16,000 B.C. The walls of caves in southwestern France and northern Spain are covered with almost life-size paintings of animals that were hunted at that time. Early hunters knew the regular migration routes of large animals such as bison and reindeer. They looked for sick or weak animals, or attacked at vulnerable moments, such as when the animals were crossing a river.

The circular calendar shows the months around the edge:

JANUARY FEBRUARY MARCH APRIL MAY JUNE JULY AUGUST SEPTEMBER OCTOBER NOVEMBER DECEMBER

THE GAME CYCLE

This illustration shows the animals people hunted in southwestern France between about 33,000 B.C. and 10,000 B.C. There was plenty of game to choose from. The hunters intercepted the animals at different times of the year as they followed their regular migration routes.

MAMMOTH HUNTERS

This woolly mammoth was carved from an animal's shoulder blade. Hunters worked in groups to kill these large mammals, one of which could feed a family for several months.

LEAP OF DEATH

In the engraving below hunters are stampeding a herd of horses over a cliff in France. The hunters probably crept up to the animals, then, at a signal, jumped to their feet, yelling to startle the herd. Skeletons of 10,000 wild horses have been found at this site.

MUSK OXEN

Today, one of the few large mammals that can survive the harsh winters of the tundra is the musk ox. Their thickset bodies have a dense covering of fur with a shaggy outer coat. During the last glacial period, musk oxen were hunted in Europe, Asia and North America.

The First Crops

I N ABOUT 8000 B.C., people in the Near East began growing their own food for the first time. Instead of simply gathering the seed of wild grasses such as wheat and barley, they saved some of it. Then, the following year, they planted it to produce a crop. As they began to control their food sources, the first farmers found that a small area of land could now feed a much larger population. People began living in permanent settlements in order to tend their crops and guard their harvest. Over the next 5000 years, farming spread from the Near East to western Asia, Europe and Africa. Farming also developed separately in other parts of Asia around 6500 B.C. and in America by about 7000 B.C.

The first farms were in hill country, where wheat and barley grew naturally, and there was enough rain for crops to grow. As populations increased, villages began to appear along river valleys, where farmers could water their crops at dry times of the year.

STONE TOOLS

This chipped flint is the blade of a hoe. It was used in North America between about A.D. 900 and A.D. 1200, but it is very similar to the hoes used by the first farmers to break up the soil. Rakes made of deer antlers were used to cover over the seeds. Ripe corn was harvested with sharp flint sickle blades.

SICKLE BLADE

This flint sickle blade has been hafted, or inserted, into a modern wooden handle. Ears of ripe corn would either have been plucked by hand or harvested with sickles such as this.

WILD RICE

Rice is a type of grass that grows in hot, damp areas such as swamps. It was a good food source for early hunter-gatherers along rivers and coasts in southern Asia. The seeds were collected when ripe and stored for use when little other food was available. The grain could be kept for many months.

WORLD CROPS

The first plants to be domesticated, or farmed, were those that grew naturally in an area. Wheat and barley grew wild in the Near East. In India, China and southeastern Asia, rice was domesticated around 5000 B.C. and soon became the main food crop. Around 3000 B.C. in Mexico, farmers grew corn, beans and squash. Farther south in the Andes mountains, the chief crops were potatoes, sweet potatoes and corn.

corn   *butternut squash*

GRINDING GRAIN

This stone quern, or hand mill, is 6000 years old. It was used to grind grain into a coarse flour for making porridge or bread. The grain was placed on the flat stone and ground into flour with the smooth, heavy rubbing stone. Flour made in this way often contained quite a lot of grit. To make bread, water was added to the flour. The mixture was then shaped into flat loaves, which were baked in a clay oven.

STRAIGHT TRACK

Several tracks were built across marshes between 4000 B.C. and 2000 B.C. in southern England. In some cases these were to link settlements to nearby fields of crops. The long, thin rods used to build the track above tell us a lot about the surrounding woodlands. The trees were coppiced, which means that thin shoots growing from cut hazel trees were harvested every few years.

A STEP UP

These terraced hillsides are in the Andes mountains of Peru. In mountainous areas where rainfall was high, some early farmers began cutting terraces, or steps, into the steep hillsides. The terraces meant that every scrap of soil could be used for planting. They prevented soil from eroding, or washing away. Farmers also used terracing to control the irrigation, or watering, of their crops. One of the first crops to be cultivated in Peru was the potato, which can be successfully grown high above sea level.

Taming Animals

ABOUT THE SAME time that people began to grow crops, they also started to domesticate (tame) wild animals. Wild sheep, goats, pigs and cattle had been hunted for thousands of years before people started to round them up into pens. Hunters may have done this to make the animals easier to catch. These animals gradually got used to people and became tamer. The first animals to be kept like this were probably sheep and goats around 8500 B.C. in the Near East.

Herders soon noticed that larger animals often had larger young. They began to allow only the finest animals to breed, so that domestic animals gradually became much stronger and larger than wild ones. Besides four-legged livestock, chickens were domesticated for their meat and also their eggs. In South America, the llama was kept for its meat and wool, along with ducks and guinea pigs. In Southeast Asia, pigs were the most important domestic animals.

WILD CATTLE
This bull is an aurochs, or wild ox. The aurochs was the ancestor of today's domestic cattle. Taming these huge, fierce animals was harder than keeping sheep and goats. Wild cattle were probably not tamed until about 7000 B.C. The aurochs became extinct in A.D. 1627. In the 1930s, a German biologist re-created the animal by crossing domesticated breeds such as Holsteins and Highland cattle.

WILD HORSES
Horses were a favorite food for prehistoric hunter-gatherers. This sculpture of a wild horse was found in Germany. It was made around 4000 B.C. Horses also often appear in cave art. They were probably first domesticated in Russia around 4400 B.C. In America, horses had become extinct through over-hunting by 9000 B.C. They were reintroduced by European explorers in the sixteenth century A.D.

DINGOES AND DOGS

The dingo is the wild dog of Australia. It is the descendant of tame dogs that were brought to the country more than 10,000 years ago by Aboriginal Australians. Dogs were the first animals to be domesticated. Their wolf ancestors were tamed to help with hunting and, later, with herding and guarding. In North America, dogs were used as pack animals and dragged a *travois* (a kind of sled) behind them.

DESERT HERDERS

Small herds of wild cattle were probably first domesticated in the Sahara and the Near East. This rock painting comes from the Tassili n'Ajjer area of the Sahara desert. It was painted in about 6000 B.C. at a time when much of the Sahara was covered by grassland and shallow lakes. The painting shows a group of herders with their cattle outside a plan of their house.

GOATS AND SHEEP

Rock paintings in the Sahara show goats and sheep, among the first animals to be domesticated. They were kept for their meat, milk, hides and wool, and are still some of the most common farmed animals.

LLAMAS

The llama was domesticated in central Peru by at least 3500 B.C. It was kept first for its meat and wool, but later it was also used for carrying food and goods long distances. A relative of the llama, the alpaca, was also domesticated for its wool.

Stone Technology

EARLY TOOLS
These chipped pebbles from Tanzania in Africa are some of the oldest tools ever found. They were made by *Homo habilis,* an early human ancestor, almost two million years ago.

S TONE AGE PEOPLE were skilled toolmakers. They used flakes of stone to make knives, spearheads, arrowheads, engraving tools (burins), piercing tools and scrapers. About two and a half million years ago, our ancestors first learned that chipping stones could give them a sharp edge. Later, they found that flint was the best stone for this. A hammerstone was used to chip off flakes of flint until the desired shape and sharpness were reached. Early tools included hand-axes, which were used for digging and cutting up animals. As people became more skillful, they made smaller tools from flakes that had been chipped off, such as chisel-like burins. These in turn were used to carve harpoons, spear-heads, needles and spear-throwers from antler and bone.

FLAKING
Neanderthals and Homosapiens were far better toolmakers than earlier people. They chipped flakes off pieces of flint to produce hand-axes (*left and middle*) and chopping tools (*right*). Pointed or oval-shaped hand-axes were used for many different tasks.

FLINT MINES
The Grimes Graves flint mine in Norfolk, England, where flint was mined from 2800 B.C. The miners traded flint with people in areas where it could not be found.

MAKE A MODEL AXE
You will need: self-drying clay, board, modeling tool, sandpaper, gray acrylic paint, dowel, craft knife, wood stain, jar of water, paintbrush, ruler, chamois leather, scissors.

1 Pull out the clay into a thick block. With a modeling tool, shape the block into an axe head with a point at one end.

2 When the clay is completely dry, lightly rub down the axe head with sandpaper to remove any rough surfaces.

3 Paint the axe head a stone color, such as gray. You could use more than one shade if you like. Leave the axe head to dry.

SPEAR POINT

The Cro-Magnons used long, thin flakes of flint to make their tools. This leaf-shaped spear point was made by highly skilled toolmakers about 20,000 years ago. Its finely flaked shape was made by delicately chipping over the entire surface.

STONES FOR TOOLS

Nodules of flint are often found in limestone rock, especially chalk, so they were reasonably easy to obtain. But other kinds of rock were used for toolmaking, too. Obsidian, a rock formed from cooled lava, was widely used in the Near East and Mexico. It fractured easily, leaving sharp edges. In parts of Africa, quartz was made into beautiful, hard-wearing hand-axes and choppers. A rock called diorite was used for making polished axe heads in Neolithic times.

quartz

chert (a type of flint)

STONE AXES

These polished stone battle axes became the most important weapon in Scandinavia by the late Neolithic period. They date from about 1800 B.C.

TOOLMAKING LESSON

Stone Age people came to depend more and more on the quality of their tools. In this reconstruction, a father is passing on his skill in toolmaking to his son.

Prehistoric people used axes for chopping wood and cutting meat. They shaped a stone blade, then attached it to a wooden shaft.

 **4** Ask an adult to trim one end of a piece of thick dowel using a craft knife. Paint the piece with wood stain and leave to dry.

5 To bind the axe head to the wooden shaft, first carefully cut a long strip of leather about an inch wide from a chamois cloth.

 **6** Place the axe head on the trimmed end of the shaft. Wrap the strip of leather around the head and shaft in a crisscross pattern.

 **7** Pull the leather strip tight and wrap the ends twice around the shaft below the head. Tie the ends together and trim them.

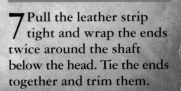

33

Carving Wood and Bone

ALTHOUGH THIS PERIOD is called the Stone Age, wood, bone, antler and ivory were just as important for making tools and other implements. Not only could these materials be carved and shaped by stone tools, but bone and antler hammers and punches were used to shape the stone tools themselves. By using these implements, better cutting edges and finer flakes of stone could be achieved.

Antler, bone, wood and ivory had many different uses. Antler picks were used to dig up roots and chip out lumps of stone. Antlers and bones were carved into spear-throwers and, along with ivory, were used to make needles, fish hooks, harpoon heads and knives. Wood was used to make the handles and mounts for spears, harpoons, axes, sickles and adzes, which were tools used for shaping wood, as well as to make bows and arrows. The shoulder blades of cattle were made into shovels, while smaller bones were used to make awls to punch small holes. Smaller bones were also used to make fine whistles and little paint holders. All these materials were often beautifully carved with animals and fine decorative patterns.

SPEAR-THROWER
This carving of a reindeer's head is probably part of a spear-thrower. Wood, bone and antler all have natural cracks and flaws in them. Prehistoric carvers often incorporated these into the design to suggest the animal's outline, as well as particular features, such as eyes, mouth and nostrils. Engraved, or carved, pictures in caves also often make use of the natural form of the rock.

ADZE
An adze was a bit like an axe, except that its blade was at right angles to the handle. The flint blade on this adze dates from about 4000 B.C. to 2000 B.C. Its wooden handle and binding are modern replacements for the originals, which have rotted away. Adzes were swung in an up-and-down movement and were used for jobs such as hollowing out tree trunks and shaping them to make dugout canoes.

AXE
Early farmers needed axes to clear land for their crops. An experiment in Denmark using a 5,000-year-old axe showed that a man could clear about $2\frac{1}{2}$ acres of woodland in about five weeks. This axe head, dating from between 4000 B.C. and 2000 B.C., has been given a modern wooden handle.

ANTLER PICK
Antlers were as useful to prehistoric humans as they were to their original owners! This tool comes from a Neolithic site near Avebury in England. Antler picks were used for digging and quarrying. Antler was a versatile material. It could be made into spear and harpoon points, needles and spear-throwers.

CRAFTSPEOPLE
This engraving shows Stone Age life as imagined by an artist from the 1800s. It shows tools being used and great care being taken over the work. Even everyday items were often finely carved and decorated by the craftspeople who made them.

CARVED BATON
This ivory object is known as a *bâton de commandment*. Several of these batons have been found, especially in France. But no one is sure what they were used for. Some experts think they were status symbols, showing the importance of the person carrying them. Others think that the holes were used to straighten arrows. Whatever their use, the batons are often decorated with fine animal carvings and geometric designs.

ANTLERS AT WORK
Two stags (male deer), fight. Only male deer have large antlers, which they use to battle with each other to win territory and females. The stags shed and grow a new set of antlers each year, so prehistoric hunters and artists had a ready supply of material.

Crafts

The very first handicraft was probably basketmaking, using river reeds and twigs woven together. Baskets were quick to make and easy to carry but not very durable. Pottery was harder-wearing. The discovery that baking clay made it stronger may have happened by accident, perhaps when a clay-lined basket fell into the fire. Baked clay figures were made from about 24,000 B.C., but it took thousands of years for people to realize that pottery could be useful for cooking and for storing food and drink. The first pots were made in Japan around 10,500 B.C. Pots were shaped from coils or lumps of clay. Their sides were smoothed and decorated before being fired in an open hearth or kiln.

Another Neolithic invention was the loom, around 6000 B.C. The first cloth was probably made of wool, cotton or flax (which could be made into linen).

BAKED-CLAY FIGURINE

This is one of the oldest fired-clay objects in the world. It is one of many similar figurines made around 24,000 B.C. at Dolni Vestonice in the Czech Republic. Here, people hunted mammoths, woolly rhinoceroses and horses. They built homes with small, oval-shaped ovens, in which they fired their figurines.

CHINESE JAR

It is amazing to think that this elegant pot was for everyday use in 4500 B.C. It was made in Banpo, near Shanghai. The people of Banpo were some of China's earliest farmers. They grew millet and kept pigs and dogs for meat. The potters made a high-quality black pottery for important occasions, and this cheaper gray pottery for everyday use.

MAKE A CLAY POT

You will need: terra-cotta modeling clay, wooden board, modeling tool, plastic flower pot, decorating tool, varnish, brush, sandpaper.

1 Roll out a long, thick sausage of clay on a wooden board. It should be at least 1/2 inch in diameter.

2 Form the roll of clay into a coil to make the base of your pot. A fairly small base can be made into a pot, a larger one into a bowl.

3 Now make a fatter roll of clay . Carefully coil this around the base to make the sides of your pot.

HOUSEHOLD POTS

Many early pots were decorated with basket-like patterns. This one has a simple geometric design and was made in Thailand around 3500 B.C. Clay pots like this were used for storing food, carrying water or cooking.

WOVEN THREADS

The earliest woven objects may have looked like this rope and cane mat from Nazca in Peru. It was made around A.D. 1000. Prehistoric people used plant-fiber rope to weave baskets and bags. The oldest known fabric dates from about 6500 B.C. and was found at Çatal Hüyük in Turkey. Few woven objects have survived, as they rot quickly.

STEATITE IDOL

Steatite, or soapstone, has been used to make this carving from the Cycladic Island of Greece. Soapstone is very soft and easy to carve. Figurines like this one were often used in funeral ceremonies. They could also be used either as the object of worship itself or as a ritual offering to a god. This figure has a cross around its neck. Although the symbol certainly has no Christian significance, no one really knows what it means.

Fired-clay pots could only be made where there were natural deposits of clay, so some areas seem to have specialized in baked-clay pottery and sculpture. The patterns used to decorate the pots vary from area to area.

4 With a modeling tool, smooth down the edges of the coil to make it flat and smooth. Make sure there are no air spaces.

5 Place your pot over a flower pot to support it. Keep adding more rolls of clay to build up the sides of your pot.

6 Smooth down the sides as you add more rolls. Then use a decorating tool with a serrated end to make different patterns.

7 Leave your pot to dry out. When the clay is dry, varnish the outside. Use sandpaper to smooth the inside of your pot.

Clothing

THE HUNTERS of the last glacial period were probably the first people to wear clothes. They needed them for protection from the cold. Clothes were made of animal hides sewn together with strips of leather. The first clothes included simple trousers, tunics and cloaks, decorated with beads of colored rock, teeth and shells. Fur boots were also worn, tied on with leather laces.

Furs were prepared by stretching out the hides and scraping them clean. The clothes were cut out and holes were made around the edges of the pieces with a sharp, pointed stone called an awl. The holes made it much easier to pass a bone needle through the hide. Cleaned hides were also used to make tents, bags and bedding.

Sometime after sheep farming began in the Near East, wool was used to weave cloth. In other parts of the world, plant fibers such as flax, cotton, bark and cactus were used. The cloth was colored and decorated with plant dyes.

PREPARING HIDES
An Inuit woman uses her teeth to soften a sealskin. Prehistoric hunter-gatherers probably also softened hides like this. Animal hides were first pegged out and scraped clean. Then they were washed and stretched taut on a wooden frame to keep them from shrinking as they dried. The stiff, dry hide was then softened and cut to shape for clothing.

PINS AND NEEDLES
These are 5000-year-old bone pins from Skara Brae in the Orkney Islands. Prehistoric people made pins and needles from slivers of bone or antler; their sides were then smoothed by rubbing them on a stone.

DYEING CLOTH
You will need: natural dyes such as walnuts, elderberries and safflower, saucepan, water, tablespoon, sieve, bowl, chamois leather, white cardboard, white T-shirt, wooden spoon. (Dyes can be found in health food shops.)

1 Choose your first dye and put approximately 8-12 tablespoons of it into an old pan. You may need to crush or shred it first.

2 Ask an adult to boil the dye, and then simmer it for one hour. Leave to cool. Pour the dye through a sieve to remove lumps.

3 Test a patch of chamois leather by dipping it in the dye for a few minutes. You can wear rubber gloves for protection.

NATURE'S COLORS

Stone Age people used the flowers, stems and leaves of many plants to make dyes. The flowers of dyer's broom and dyer's chamomile gave a range of colors from bright yellow to khaki. Plants such as woad and indigo gave a rich blue dye, while the bark, leaves and husks of the walnut made a deep brown. Plants were also used to prepare hides. Skins were then softened by being soaked with oak bark in water.

dyer's broom

birch bark

oak bark

RAW MATERIALS

This engraving shows an Inuit man hunting a seal in the Arctic. Animals provided skin for cloth, sinews for thread and bones for needles. Clothes made of animal skin kept out the cold and rain, and allowed early people to live farther north.

KEEPING WARM

This Nenet woman from Siberia in Russia is wearing a reindeer-skin coat called a *yagushka*. Prehistoric people probably dressed in a similar way to keep out the cold. Waterproof pants, hooded parkas, boots and mittens would have been worn.

GRASS SOCKS

Until recently the Inuit of North America gathered grasses in summer and braided them into socks like these. The socks were shaped to fit the foot snugly and were worn under sealskin boots.

4 Lay the patch on a piece of white cardboard and leave it to dry. Be careful not to drip the dye over clothes as you work.

5 Make up the other two dyes and test them out in the same way. Compare the patches and choose your favorite color.

6 Dye a white T-shirt by soaking it in your chosen dye. Try to make sure that the T-shirt is dyed evenly all over.

Safflower flowers for dyeing were picked when first open, then dried.

Ornament and Decoration

CEREMONIAL DRESS
The amazing headdress, face painting and jewelry still seen at ceremonies in Papua New Guinea may echo the richness of decoration in Stone Age times.

B OTH MEN AND WOMEN wore jewelry in the Stone Age. Necklaces and pendants were made from all sorts of natural objects. Brightly colored pebbles, snail shells, fish bones, animal teeth, seashells, eggshells, nuts and seeds were all used. Later, semiprecious amber and jade, fossilized jet and handmade clay beads were also used. The beads were threaded onto thin strips of leather or twine made from plant fibers.

Other jewelry included bracelets made of slices of elephant or mammoth tusk. Strings of shells and teeth were made into beautiful headbands. Women braided their hair and put it up with combs and pins. People probably decorated their bodies and outlined their eyes with pigments such as red ochre. They may have tattooed and pierced their bodies, too.

BODY PAINT
These Australian Aboriginal children have painted their bodies with clay. They have used patterns that are thousands of years old.

BONES AND TEETH
This necklace is made from the bones and teeth of a walrus. It comes from Skara Brae in the Orkney Islands. A hole was made in each bead with a stone tool, or with a wooden stick spun by a bow drill. The beads were then strung onto a strip of leather or twine.

MAKE A NECKLACE
You will need: self-drying clay, rolling pin and board, modeling tool, sandpaper, ivory and black acrylic paint, paintbrush, water, ruler, scissors, chamois leather, cardboard, double-sided tape, white glue, leather laces.

1 Roll out the clay on a board and cut out four crescent shapes with the modeling tool. Leave them on the board to dry.

2 Rub the crescents lightly with sandpaper and paint them an ivory color. You could varnish them later to make them shiny.

3 Cut four strips of leather 4 inches by 1 1/2 inches. Use the edge of a piece of cardboard to make a black crisscross pattern on the strips.

NATURAL DECORATION

We know about the wide variety of materials used in Stone Age jewelry from cave paintings and ornaments discovered in graves. Shells were highly prized and some were traded over long distances. Other materials included deers' teeth, mammoth and walrus ivory, fish bones and birds' feathers.

a selection of seashells

A WARRIOR'S HEADDRESS

This Yali warrior from Indonesia has a headdress of wild boars' teeth and a necklace made of shells and bone. Headdresses and necklaces made of animals' teeth may have had a spiritual meaning for Stone Age people. The wearer may have believed that the teeth brought the strength or courage of the animal from which they came.

BANGLES AND EAR STUDS

This jewelry comes from Harappa in Pakistan. It dates from between 2300 B.C. and 1750 B.C. and is made from shells and coloured pottery. Archaeologists in Harappa have found the remains of dozens of shops that sold jewelry.

Stone Age people believed that wearing a leopard-claw necklace brought them magical powers.

4 When they are dry, fold back the edges of each strip and hold in place with double-sided sticky tape.

5 Brush the middle of each crescent with glue and wrap the leather around, forming a loop at the top, as shown.

6 Braid together three leather laces to make a thong. Make the thong long enough to go around your neck and be tied.

7 Thread the leopard's claws onto the middle of the thong, arranging them so that there are small spaces between them.

The Arts

STONE AGE ARTISTS were wonderfully skilled, working in stone, antler, bone, ivory and clay. They painted rock walls, engraved stone and ivory and carved musical instruments. They created images of the animals they hunted, as well as human figures and abstract designs. No one knows for sure why they were so creative.

The earliest works of art date from around 40,000 B.C. and were etched onto rocks in Australia. In Europe, the oldest works of art are cave paintings from about 28,000 B.C. Most cave paintings, however, date from around 16,000 B.C. The walls of caves in northern Spain and southwestern France are covered with paintings and engravings of animals. Stone Age artists also carved female figures, called Venus figurines, and decorated their tools and weapons. This explosion in art ended around 10,000 B.C.

VENUS FIGURINES
This small figure, called the Venus of Lespugue, was found in France. It dates from about 20,000 B.C. Her full figure probably represents the fertility of a goddess. She may have been carried as a good luck charm.

MUSIC AND DANCE
Stone Age rock paintings in Europe and Africa show people moving in dance-like patterns. This engraving from a cave on the island of Sicily dates from about 9000 B.C. Ceremonies in the Stone Age almost certainly included music and dancing, perhaps with drums and whistles, too.

MAKE A CAVE PAINTING
You will need: self-drying craft clay, rolling pin and board, modeling tool, sandpaper, acrylic paints, paintbrush, jar of water.

1 First roll out the craft clay, giving it a slightly bumpy surface like a cave wall. Cut it into a neat shape with a modeling tool.

2 When the clay has dried, lightly rub down the surface with sandpaper to make it smooth and give a good surface to paint on.

3 Paint the outline of your chosen animal in black. This painting shows a reindeer similar to those in Stone Age cave paintings.

EARLY POTTERY

These two female figures are some of the earliest surviving South American ceramics (baked pottery). They date from about 4000 B.C. to 1800 B.C. Their distinctive shape and fringed hair means they were made by people of the Valdivia culture. It seems that in some parts of the world, pottery was shaped into statuettes long before it was used to make storage vessels and cooking pots for food.

AN ARTIST'S MATERIALS

Prehistoric artists made their paints from soft rocks and minerals such as charcoal and clay. They ground these to a powder and mixed them with water or animal fat. Charcoal from the fire was used for black outlines and shading. Colored earth, called ocher, gave browns, reds and yellows. A clay called kaolin was used for white paint. The paint was stored in hollow bones. Brushes were made from animal hair, moss or frayed twigs.

ocher   *charcoal*

SPIRAL DESIGNS

These carved stones are from the temple at Tarxien on the island of Malta and date from around 2500 B.C. Many large stone monuments that were built in Europe around 4200 B.C. are decorated with geometric patterns.

4 Draw the most obvious features of your animal by exaggerating their size. The sweeping horns of this deer make it very striking.

5 When the outline is dry, mix yellow, red and black to make a warm color with which to fill in the outline of your animal.

6 Finish off your picture by highlighting some parts of the body with reddish brown paint mixed to resemble red ochre.

Stone Age artists painted in black, white and earthy colors.

Trade and Distribution

STONE AGE PEOPLE did not use bills and coins for money, as we do. Instead they bartered, or exchanged, things. When one person wanted a bowl, for example, he or she had to offer something in exchange to the owner of the bowl—perhaps a tool or ornament. Toward the end of the Stone Age, however, people began to use shells or stone rings as a kind of currency.

Even isolated hunter-gatherer groups came into contact with each other and exchanged things, such as seashells for tools or hides. With the beginning of farming around 8000 B.C. in the Near East, however, long-distance exchange and a more organized trading system began. New activities, such as farming, pottery and weaving, needed specialized tools, so a high value was put on suitable rocks. In western Europe, flint quarries produced axe blades that were prized and traded over enormous distances. Sometimes goods were traded thousands of miles from where they were made.

COWRIE SHELLS
Small, highly polished cowrie shells were popular as decoration for clothes and jewelry in prehistoric times. The shells have been found scattered around skeletons in burial sites, many of which are hundreds of miles from the coast. Later, cowrie shells were used as money in Africa and parts of Asia.

AXES
A good, strong axe was a valuable commodity. It was particularly important for early farmers, who used it to chop down trees and clear land for crops. Axe heads made of special stone were traded over wide distances.

BURIED WITH WEALTH
This communal burial on the Solomon Islands in the Pacific Ocean shows the deceased surrounded by shells and ornaments. Shells have been used for money for thousands of years—in fact, for longer and over a wider area than any currency, including coins. One hoard of shells, found in Iraq, was dated before 18,000 B.C.

STONE TRADE

During the neolithic period there was a widespread trade in stone for axes. At Graig Llywd in Wales (*left*), stone was quarried from the scree slopes and taken all over Britain. The blades were roughed out on site, then transported to other parts of the country, where they were ground and polished into axe heads. Rough, unfinished axes have been found lying on the ground at Graig.

FUR TRAPPER

A modern Cree trapper from the Canadian Arctic is surrounded by his catch of pine marten pelts. Furs were almost certainly a valuable commodity for prehistoric people, especially for hunter-gatherers trading with more settled farmers. They could be traded for food or precious items such as amber or tools.

SKINS AND PELTS

White Arctic fox skins are left to dry in the cold air. In winter, Arctic foxes grow a thick white coat so that they are well camouflaged against the snow. Furs like these have traditionally been particularly valuable to Arctic people, both for the clothing that makes Arctic life possible and for trading.

Transport on Land and Sea

The EARLIEST MEANS of transport, besides traveling on foot, was by boat. The first people to reach Australia, perhaps as early as 50,000 B.C., must have used log or bamboo rafts to cross open water. Later, skin-covered coracles and kayaks (canoes hollowed from tree trunks) and boats made from reeds were used. On land, people dragged goods on wooden sledges or *travois* (triangular platforms of poles lashed together). Logs were used as rollers to move heavy loads. The taming of horses, donkeys and camels in about 4000 B.C. revolutionized land transport. The first roads and causeways in Europe were built around the same time. Around 3500 B.C., the wheel was invented by metal-using people in Mesopotamia. It quickly spread to Stone Age people in Europe.

HORSE'S HEAD
This rock engraving of a horse's head comes from a cave in France. Some experts think that horses may have been tamed as early as 12,000 B.C. There are carvings that appear to show bridles around the heads of horses, but the marks may indicate manes.

CORACLE
A man fishes from a coracle, one of the oldest boat designs. Made of animal hide stretched over a wooden frame, the coracle may have been used since around 7600 B.C.

MAKE A MODEL CANOE
You will need: cardboard, pencil, ruler, scissors, white glue, glue brush, masking tape, self-drying clay, double-sided tape, chamois leather, compass, thread, needle.

canoe top
— 8in —
canoe top
— 4in —
canoe base
— 8in —
canoe base
— 4in —

1 Cut cardboard to the size of the templates shown on the left. Remember to cut semicircles from the long edge of both top pieces.

2 Glue the bases together and the tops together, using masking tape to secure them as they dry. Join the top to the base in the same way.

STONE BRIDGE

Walla Brook bridge on Dartmoor is one of the oldest stone bridges in Britain. Bridges make traveling easier, safer and more direct. The first bridges were made by placing tree trunks across rivers, or by laying flat stones in shallow streams.

SAILING BOATS

This is a model of a skin-covered boat called an *umiak,* which was used by the Inuit of North America. The figure at the back is the helmsman, whose job is to steer the boat. The other figures are rowing the oars. The ancient Egyptians seem to have been the first people to use sailing ships, around 3200 B.C.

KAYAK FRAME

This wooden frame for a kayak was made by an Inuit fisherman. It has been built without any nails; the joints are lashed together with strips of leather. Canoes such as this have been in use for thousands of years.

Inuit kayaks give clues about how Stone Age boats may have looked. The outsides were covered with skin.

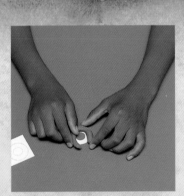

3 Draw three circles the size of the holes in the top, with a smaller circle inside each. Cut them out and make rings the same size from modeling clay.

4 Cover the modeling-clay and the cardboard rings with double-sided tape. These rings form the seats where the paddlers would sit.

5 Cover your canoe with chamois leather, leaving holes for the seats. Glue the leather tightly in place so that all cardboard is covered.

6 Use a needle and thread to sew up the edges of the leather on the top of the canoe. Position and attach the seats and the oars.

Warfare and Weapons

WARFARE AND FIGHTING were certainly a part of Stone Age life. Prehistoric skeletons often reveal wounds received during a fight. For example, in a cemetery in Egypt dating from about 12,000 B.C., the skeletons of 58 men, women and children have been found, many with the flint flakes that killed them still stuck in their bones. In South Africa, a rare rock engraving, dating from between 8000 B.C. and 3000 B.C., shows two groups of people fighting each other with bows and arrows. No one knows exactly why these people fought each other. After 8000 B.C., as the population of farmers grew, conflict between farming groups competing for land increased. Early farming villages were often encircled by earthworks, mud-brick walls or high wooden fences for protection.

AMERICAN POINT
This type of stone weapon was used by hunter-gatherers in North America to hunt bison. It is called a Folsom point and dates from around 8000 B.C.

DEADLY ARROWHEADS
The first arrowheads may have been made of wood, hardened over a fire. Yet flint could be given a much sharper edge. This hoard was found in Brittany, France. Sharp weapons could mean the difference between life and death, so they were very valuable.

A BOW AND ARROW
You will need: self-drying clay, rolling pin and board, modeling tool, sandpaper, acrylic paint, paintbrush, two lengths of thin dowel (16 inches and 24 inches), craft knife, double-sided tape, scissors, string.

1 Roll out the craft clay and use a modeling tool to cut out an arrowhead shape. When dry, smooth with sandpaper and paint gray.

2 Ask an adult to trim down one end of the shorter length of dowel with a craft knife. This is the arrow shaft.

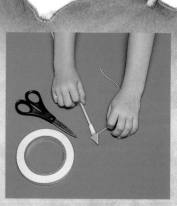

3 Tape the arrowhead to the shaft with double-sided tape. Wrap string around the tape to imitate leather binding.

VIOLENT DEATH

Many people in Stone Age times met with violent deaths. This skull contains an arrow point that entered through the unlucky victim's nostrils, presumably during a fight.

HUNTERS OR WARRIORS?

By about 13,000 B.C., prehistoric hunters had learned that bows and arrows were more powerful and accurate than spears. This rock painting, dating from around 6000 B.C., shows hunters or warriors with bows and arrows out on a raid.

BLADES AND POINTS

A selection of flint arrowheads and knife blades from Egypt shows fine workmanship. Flakes of flint about 8 inches long were used as lance heads. Shorter ones were made into javelins, knives and arrows. The heads were mounted onto wooden shafts with tree-resin glue and strips of leather.

Prehistoric hunter-gatherers carried small, lightweight bows from which they could fire many arrows quickly.

 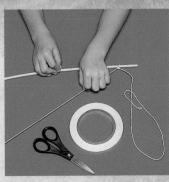  

4 Use the longer length of dowel to make the bow. Tie a long length of string securely to one end of the bow.

5 Ask an adult to help you carefully bend back the bow and tie the string to the other end. Tape will help to secure the string.

6 To tighten and secure the bowstring further, wind the string around each end several time. Then tie it and cut off the end.

7 Using double-sided tape, wrap another piece of string around the middle of the bow as a rest for the arrow.

Religion and Magic

WE CAN ONLY GUESS at the beliefs of Stone Age people. The first people we know of who buried their dead were the Neanderthals. This suggests that they believed in a spirit world. Early people probably worshipped the spirits of the animals they hunted and other natural things. Some paintings and engravings on rocks and in caves may have a magical or religious purpose. Small statues, called Venus figurines, were probably worshipped as goddesses of fertility or plenty. Prehistoric people probably thought illnesses and accidents were caused by evil spirits. It may have been the job of one person, called a shaman, to speak to the spirits and interpret what should be done.

As farming spread and settlements grew into towns, more organized religions began. Shrines decorated with religious pictures have been found at Çatal Hüyük in Turkey, the site of a well-preserved town dating from around 7000 B.C.

ANCIENT BURIAL
The skull of the skeleton from this burial found in France has been scattered with red ocher earth. Red may have represented blood or life for Stone Age people. Bodies were often buried on their sides, with their knees pulled up to their chins. Tools, ornaments, food and weapons were put in the graves. Later Stone Age people built elaborate tombs for their dead.

RITUAL ANTLERS
These antlers are from a red stag and were found at Star Carr in England. Some experts think that antlers were worn by a kind of priest called a shaman, perhaps in a coming-of-age ceremony or to bring good luck in that season's hunt.

CLAY GODDESS
This female figure is made from clay and was found at Pazardzik in Bulgaria. Many prehistoric societies worshipped images of the earth goddess, or great mother. As the mother of the world, she gave life to plants, animals and humans, and so ensured the future of the human race.

TREPANNING

Cutting a hole in a person's head is called trepanning. It was practiced in prehistoric times from about 5000 B.C. A sharp flint tool was used to cut a hole in the skull in order to let illness escape from the body. Several skulls have been found showing the hole starting to close—evidence that some patients survived this blood-curdling procedure!

SPELLS AND POTIONS

In many hunter-gatherer societies today, a shaman (witch doctor) can speak with the spirits from the world of the dead. In cultures such as that of the Amazonian Indians shamans also administer potions from plants to cure illness. They use plants such as quinine, coca and curare. Stone Age people probably developed similar preparations. There is evidence that neolithic farmers in northwestern Europe grew poppies and hemp, possibly for use in magic potions and rituals.

poppy

ANCESTOR WORSHIP

This skull comes from Jericho in the Near East and dates from about 6500 B.C. Before the people of Jericho buried their dead, they removed the skulls. These were covered with plaster and painted to look like the features of the dead person. Cowrie shells were used for eyes. Some experts believe that this was done as a form of ancestor worship.

RITUAL DANCE

A modern painting shows a traditional Australian Aboriginal dance. Ceremonies are an important part of Aboriginal life, and evidence of similar rituals has also been found at prehistoric sites in Australia. Aboriginal beliefs are designed to maintain the delicate balance between people and their environment.

Monuments of Wood and Stone

THE FIRST GREAT STONE MONUMENTS were built in Europe and date from around 4200 B.C. They are called megaliths (which means "large stones" in Greek) and were built by early farming communities from Scandinavia to the Mediterranean. Some of the first megaliths were dolmens, made up of a large, flat stone supported by several upright stones. They are the remains of ancient burial places, called chambered tombs; they may also have been used to mark a community's territory. Some are called passage graves; these were communal graves, where many people were buried. Later, larger monuments were constructed. Wood or stone circles called henges, such as Stonehenge in England, were built. No one knows why these circles were made—they may have been temples, meeting places or giant calendars, since they are aligned with the sun, moon and stars.

DOLMEN
The bare stones shown here are all that is left of a chambered tomb once covered by a large mound of earth. This configuration of stones, called a dolmen, once surrounded a burial chamber.

WOODEN HENGE
This is a modern reconstruction of a wooden henge (circle) excavated at Sarn-y-Brn-Caled in Wales. People started building wooden henges around 3000 B.C. Henges were centers of religious and social life.

A WOODEN HENGE
You will need: cardboard, ruler, compass, pencil, scissors, terra-cotta clay, rolling pin and board, modeling tool, 1/2in- and 1/5in-thick dowel, sandpaper, acrylic paint, paintbrush, fake grass, white glue, wood stain, brush.

1 Cut out a circle of card about 14 inches in diameter. Roll out the clay, place the circle on top and cut around the clay.

2 Press a 1/2inch-thick stick around the edge to make a ring of evenly spaced post holes. Mark a circle, about 4 inches across, inside the first.

3 Press the stick around the second circle to make 5 evenly spaced holes. Leave the base to dry. Sand it and paint it brown.

STONE TEMPLE

This is Hgar Quim temple on the island of Malta. Many stone temples were built on Malta between 3600 B.C. and 2500 B.C. The oldest have walls at least 20 feet long and 11½ feet tall. The most impressive temple is the Hypogeum, carved on three levels, deep underground.

STANDING STONES

Stonehenge was built over many centuries from about 2800 B.C. to 1400 B.C. The first Stonehenge was a circular earthwork made up of a bank and ditch. Later, large blocks of dressed (shaped) sarsen stones were put up. The stones are aligned with the midsummer sunrise and midwinter sunset, as well as the positions of the moon.

PASSAGE GRAVE

This stone lies at the entrance to a passage grave at Newgrange in Ireland. The grave is a circular mound with a single burial chamber at the center, reached by a long passage. Many of the stone slabs that line the passage are decorated with spirals and circles.

4 Cover the base with uneven pieces of fake grass, glued into place. Be careful not to completely cover up the post holes.

5 Cut short sticks for the posts and lintels. Cut 7 more longer sticks. Paint the sticks with wood stain and leave to dry.

6 Glue the sticks in place using the post holes as guides. When dry, glue the lintels on top to complete your wood circle.

Wood henges, or circles, had up to five rings of timber posts, increasing in height toward the center.

53

Journey Through Life

STONE AGE PEOPLE held ceremonies to mark the significant stages in their lives, such as birth, coming of age, marriage and death. Coming-of-age ceremonies marked the point when boys and girls were thought of as adults, playing a full part in the life of the clan. Life spans in Stone Age times were much shorter than they are today. Old people were valued members of the clan, as they were able to pass on their skills and knowledge. Most people lived into their thirties, but few survived into their sixties. There was little people could do fight illness and infection, and many infants died at birth. When game and food were plentiful, however, it seems that hunter-gatherers probably had an easier way of life than later farmers, whose work was hard and unending.

BURIAL SCENE
This burial from northeastern France was made in about 4500 B.C. at the time when farming was starting in that area. These farmers were buried in small cemetries, often with shell ornaments, adzes, and stones for grinding grain.

DOGGU FIGURE
This Jomon human figurine from Japan was made of clay between 2500 B.C. and 1000 B.C. These figurines were often used during funerary rituals and, in some cases, were also buried in graves.

A PASSAGE GRAVE

You will need: cardboard, compass and pencil, ruler, scissors, rolling pin and board, terra-cotta self-drying clay, modeling tool, white self-drying clay, white glue and glue brush, rich soil, spoon, green fabric.

1 Cut out two cardboard circles, with diameters of 8 inches and 10 inches. Roll out the clay and cut around the larger circle with a modeling tool.

2 Put the smaller circle on top of the larger circle and cover it with clay. With a modeling tool, mark out the passage and chamber.

3 Roll out the white clay and cut it into squares. Form rocks from some squares and model the rest into stone slabs.

FAMILY GRAVE

This tomb at West Kennet in southern England was built around 3700 B.C. It was used for ceremonies involving the dead. The stone chambers inside the barrow (mound of earth) contain the bones of at least 46 people. The corpses were not placed inside the barrow right away, but were first left outside until most of the flesh had rotted away. Then the skeletons were disarticulated (divided up) and the bones placed in the tomb. Some of the skulls and long bones were removed, perhaps for a ceremony somewhere else. The barrow was blocked up and reopened many times over the thousand years it was in use.

burial chamber

barrow

entrance

Ditches dug around the outside of a barrow provided the soil to build the mound. Many people could be buried together in a burial site like this one.

4 When the clay is dry, build the walls and roof of the passage and chamber. Glue the slabs carefully in place.

5 Spoon soil gently over the chamber, heaping it up to make a large, even mound. Do not press on the clay chamber.

6 Cut out a piece of green fabric large enough to cover the mound of soil. Dip the fabric in glue and position it gently.

7 Place clay boulders all around the edge of the earthwork. When you are happy with their positions, glue them in place.

Neolithic Villages

WHEN PEOPLE took up farming as a way of life, it meant that they had to stay in the same place for a long time. In some areas, farmers practiced slash and burn. This means they cleared land, but moved on after a few years when their crops had exhausted the soil. Elsewhere, early farming settlements grew into villages five to ten times bigger than earlier hunter-gatherer camps. At first, the farmers still hunted wild animals and foraged for food, but soon their herds and crops supplied most of their needs. They lived in villages of rectangular or circular one-story houses of stone, mud-brick, or timber and thatch. The houses were joined by narrow lanes or courtyards. Most villages lay on low ground, near well-watered, easily worked land. By using irrigation and crop rotation, later farmers were able to stay in one place for a long time.

INSIDE A LONG HOUSE
The inside of a long house was a place of work as well as a shelter for the family and their animals. Around the hearth of this reconstructed house are baskets woven from reeds, and skins laid out on the floor. Around the walls, tools are stored.

A LONG HOUSE
This is a reconstruction of a typical long house in an early farming village in Europe. The village dates from around 4500 B.C.

A TOWN HOUSE

This picture shows how the inside of a house at Çatal Hüyük in Turkey may have looked. The walls were made of mud-brick, with poles covered with reeds and mud as the roof. All the houses were joined together, with no streets in between. People got around by climbing over the rooftops and entering their homes by a ladder through the roof.

The main room of each house had raised areas for sitting and sleeping. More than a thousand houses were packed together like this at Çatal Hüyük.

THE OVEN

Many houses contained ovens or kilns, used for baking bread and firing pottery. A kiln allowed higher temperatures to be reached than an open hearth, and therefore produced better pottery. Each village probably made its own pottery.

STONE WALLS

These are the remains of the walls of a house in an early farming village in Jordan. It was built around 7000 B.C. The walls are made of stone collected from the local area. The first farming towns and villages appeared in the Near East. Most were built of mud-brick and, over hundreds of years, such settlements were often rebuilt many times on the same site.

The End of an Era

THE END OF the Stone Age was marked by the growth of towns and cities. The very first town was probably Jericho in the Near East. In about 8000 B.C., a farming village was built there on the site of an earlier settlement. By about 7800 B.C., nearly 2700 people lived in Jericho. Çatal Hüyük in Turkey was the site of another, much larger town, dating from about 6500 B.C. and with a population of about 5000. The people who lived in these towns were not just farmers—they were also craftspeople, priests and traders. When metalworking became widespread, better tools allowed people to produce more food. Improved farming led to the first civilizations, with well-organized workforces, armies and governments ruled by kings and priests. These civilizations grew up in the fertile areas of Mesopotamia, Egypt, India and China, heralding the end of the Stone Age.

A Slim Figurine
This female figurine was made around 2000 B.C. on the Cycladic Islands of Greece. Her slender shape contrasts greatly with the fuller figures of earlier female statuettes. She may have been created as a continuation of the tradition of fertility figurines, or mother goddesses, in new, town-based societies.

Jericho
In about 8000 B.C., farmers built a settlement at Jericho in the Near East. It was surrounded by a ditch and massive stone walls. The walls were broken by a great round tower, the remains of which are shown here. The people of Jericho traded with bands of nomadic hunter-gatherers.

Make a Figurine
You will need: board, terra-cotta self-drying clay, modeling tool, glass tumbler, white glue (mixed with water for varnish) and brush.

1 First, mold a flattish, triangular shape from craft clay to form the body. Then roll out a fat sausage for the arms and legs.

2 Trim two lengths from the sausage to form the arms. Then cut the rest of the sausage to form two leg pieces.

3 Attach the arms to the body, smoothing down the seam and marking the shoulder area lightly with a modeling tool.

SARGON OF AKKAD

This Sumerian carving dates from about 2300 B.C. and depicts Sargon, king of Akkad. Sumer was the first civilization in the world. It arose in southern Mesopotamia (modern Iraq) in about 3200 B.C. The Sumerians were great traders.

REFINED POTTERY

This beautiful pottery jar is from the Jomon period in Japan and was made around 3000 B.C. The Japanese were making pottery as early as 10,500 B.C., and their Jomon culture thrived until as late as 300 B.C. Clay continued to be, and still is, an important material for the manufacture of ceramics.

WEIGHTS AND MEASURES

As trade grew, people needed a fair system of weights and measures. These weights and scales come from the city of Mohenjo-Daro, a center of the Harrapan civilization in Pakistan.

A prehistoric clay figure similar to this one has been nicknamed "The Thinker." It was made in Romania around 5200 B.C.

4 Roll out a piece of clay for the neck and a ball for the head. Sculpt features onto the face. Attach the head and neck to the body.

5 Lean the figure against a glass to support it. Attach the legs, molding the feet by pinching the ends of the rolls, as shown.

6 Bend each arm in turn and position so that the hands support the figurine's head and the elbows rest on its knees.

7 Leave the clay to dry, then gently remove the glass. Varnish the figurine lightly and leave it to dry again before moving it.

The Stone Age Today

THE SPREAD OF METALWORKING and farming changed the way people lived, but only very slowly. Huge areas of the world continued to live in the Stone Age. In many areas, people continued to live a hunter-gatherer way of life even when they knew about farming methods. In addition, large parts of the world remained isolated from each other until quite recently. Without the use of metal, Stone Age people evolved into complicated and advanced societies of their own. Incredibly, by 1000 B.C., people from southeastern Asia had colonized many of the Pacific islands, crossing up to 400 miles of open ocean. This was a great deal farther than people elsewhere had dared to travel without being in sight of land. Stone Age societies have survived right up to the twentieth century. The Inuit of the Arctic, the Aborigines of Australia and the San hunter-gatherers of southern Africa continue to preserve a way of life that is thousands of years old.

ARCTIC PEOPLES

This is a Nenet man from Siberia in Russia. The Nenet share a traditional way of life with the Inuit of North America. Today, most live in small settlements or towns, but they are very proud of their culture. They preserve their own language, art and songs, and regard hunting as an essential part of their way of life.

PAPUA NEW GUINEA

These men are taking part in one of the spectacular traditional dances of Papua New Guinea. The highland areas of Papua New Guinea have formed a natural barrier between different groups of people. This has helped to preserve a rich variety of cultures and languages. Many people in small villages continue to grow their own food and hunt for animals in the dense forests.

ABORIGINAL AUSTRALIANS

In Australia today, 200 years after the arrival of Europeans, some Aboriginal people are trying to maintain a traditional way of life. Thousands of years ago, their ancestors must have been well aware of how to grow plants such as yams, but they chose to continue as hunter-gatherers. In tune with their environment, they had a wide range of game and food plants available to them, making farming an unnecessary and more difficult way of life.

MARVELS IN STONE

Gigantic stone heads up to 40 feet high were carved out of volcanic rock and erected on Easter Island between A.D. 1100 and A.D. 1600. Easter Island is one of the most remote islands in the Pacific.

STONEMASONS

This is part of an illustration dating from the fifteenth century A.D., showing medieval stonemasons at work. Large workforces and metal tools gradually helped stone to take on a new role as a building material. Stone could be cut, shaped and transported on a much larger scale. Many impressive stone buildings were erected all over the world, some of which have stood for thousands of years.

Glossary

A

adze A tool for cutting away wood. It has a blade at right angles to the handle.

ancestor A member of the same family who died long ago.

archaeology The scientific study of the past looking at the things people left behind, such as tools.

Australopithecus (southern ape) An ape-like ancestor of human beings. The first hominid to walk upright.

awl A small, pointed tool, used for making holes in hides.

B

barter The exchange of goods, one for the other.

bow drill A tool used to drill holes in bone and shell, and also to generate heat to make fire.

burin A chisel-like flint tool.

bow drill

C

clan A group of people related to each other by ancestry or marriage.

coppice A managed wood in which the tree shoots are cut off in order to encourage new growth.

coracle A small, round boat made of wickerwork and covered with watertight material.

Cro-Magnons The first modern humans to live in Europe.

cuneiform The first system of writing. It was invented by the Sumerians of Mesopotamia.

dugout canoe

D

dolmen The remains of a tomb made of a large flat stone laid on top of several upright stones.

dugout canoe A type of canoe made by hollowing out a tree trunk.

E

earthwork A bank of earth that was built like a defensive wall around a settlement.

evolution The changes that take place in an animal or plant species over millions of years, as it becomes more complex.

extinction The complete disappearance, or death, of a whole species of animals or plants.

F

fertility goddess A goddess believed to give life to all plants, animals and humans.

flax A plant with stringy stems that are used to make linen cloth.

flint A hard stone. It flakes easily, creating sharp edges used to make tools and weapons.

G

glacial A period in the earth's history when a large area of the world was covered by ice.

H

haft The handle of an axe or knife.

(continued)

hand-axe A heavy tool that fitted into the palm of the hand and had sharp edges.

henge A circular monument made of wood or stone named after Stonehenge in England.

hominid Humans and their most recent ancestors.

Homo erectus (upright man) The first humans to use fire and shelter to live in cooler climates.

Homo habilis (handy man) The first humans to make tools.

Homo sapiens (wise man) The species to which all modern humans and the Neanderthals belong.

hunter-gatherer Person whose way of life involves hunting wild animals and gathering plant foods.

L

land bridge A strip of land, often revealed by falling sea levels, that joins two land masses.

M

mammoth An extinct member of the elephant family that lived on open plains.

mastodon An extinct elephant-like animal that lived in the forest.

megalith A large stone monument.

mammoth

Neanderthal woman

Mesolithic (Middle Stone Age) A period that began about 12,000 years ago and ended with the spread of farming.

Mesopotamia The fertile region between the Tigris and Euphrates rivers, where the world's first cities grew up.

N

Neanderthals A group of Homo sapiens who were the first people to bury their dead.

Neolithic (New Stone Age) A period that began about 10,000 years ago and lasted until metal-working became widespread.

nomad A member of a group that roams from place to place.

O

ochre A type of yellow- or red-coloured earth used as pigment (colour) in paint.

P

Palaeolithic (Old Stone Age) A period that began about 2 million years ago when the first stone tools were made.

passage grave A communal grave made up of an earth mound with a long passage leading to the stone chamber at its centre.

prehistoric Belonging to the time before written records were made.

Q

quern A hand-mill used for grinding corn.

R

radiocarbon dating A very accurate method of dating objects.

S

shaman A medicine man or woman with powers to heal and contact spirits.

sickle A tool with a curved blade used to harvest crops.

sinew An animal tendon joining muscle to bone. It was used by prehistoric people as sewing thread.

tally stick

spear-thrower A tool that acted as an extension of the arm, to give extra leverage for throwing spears.

species A group of animals (or plants) of the same kind that breed and produce offspring.

symbol A mark in a painting or on a stone that has a special meaning.

T

tally stick A piece of wood or bone, cut with notches in order to record the number of items or days.

tepee A conical tent, home of nomadic Native Americans.

tinder Dry material that quickly catches fire if a spark falls on it.

trade The exchange of goods in order to make money.

travois A platform for baggage formed by poles roped together. It was dragged by a person or tied to the back of a dog or horse.

trepanning Cutting a hole in a person's head. It was practised in prehistoric times in order to let illness escape from the body.

tribe A group of people that shared a common language and way of life.

tundra A treeless area where the soil is permanently frozen under the surface. Harsh winters are followed by a short summer growing season.

U

umiak A rowing boat made from whalebone, covered with walrus hide and waterproofed with seal oil. It had a single sail and was used by the Inuit people to hunt whales.

V

Venus figurine A small statue of a woman, usually shown with large hips, breasts and buttocks, and with a full stomach. The figurines may have been worshipped as symbols of fertility or plenty, or carried as good luck charms.

W

witchetty grub A goat moth larva, eaten by Aboriginal Australians.

woolly rhinoceros A kind of extinct prehistoric mammal.

Venus figurine

Index

A

Aboriginal Australians 40, 51, 60-61
animal domestication 6-9, 11, 13, 30-3
animal skins and furs 38-9, 45, 56
antlers 5, 12, 22, 26, 32, 34, 35, 38, 42, 50
arts and crafts 5, 16-17, 32, 34, 35, 36-37, 42-3
Australopithecus 8-9
axes 5, 26, 32-4, 44

B

Bering Strait 6, 7, 11
bison 4, 10, 11, 25, 26
boats and ships 7, 8, 46-7
body decoration 40-41
bone 4, 5, 16, 18-19, 24, 26, 27, 32, 34-5, 39, 42
bow drills 20-21
bows and arrows 26, 32, 48-9
building 9, 18-19, 56-7, 61
burial 4, 8, 9, 37, 41, 44, 48, 50-55

C

camps 12-13
canoes 7, 46-7
carvings 5, 26, 27
Çatal Hüyük 7, 37, 50, 57, 58
cattle 7, 15, 30-31
cave art 4, 5, 11, 16-17, 20, 26, 34, 41, 42-3, 50
caves 5, 18
climate 5, 10-13, 24
cloth 13, 36, 38
clothing 26, 36, 38-9
communication 16-17
cooking 21, 22-3
counting 16-17
Cro-Magnon people 4, 8, 33
cuneiform 9, 16-17
Cycladic Islands 15, 37, 58

D

dance 42, 51
deer 10, 12, 35
diet 22-3
dolmens 52
dyeing 38-9

E

engravings 5, 32, 34, 42-3, 46, 48, 50

F

farming 6-9, 12, 28-9, 38, 48, 50-51, 54, 56, 60
fire 8, 9, 20-21, 36-7, 48
fishing 24-5, 34
flint 8-9, 28, 32-4, 44, 48-9
flour 6, 15, 29
food crops 6-9, 12, 28-9

G

glacials 6, 10-11, 26
Grimes Graves 9, 32
grindstones 6, 29

H

Harappa 41, 59
harpoons 12, 24-5, 32, 34, 35
henges 9, 52-3
herders 12, 13, 31
Homo Australopithecus 8
Homo erectus 4, 8-9, 20
Homo habilis 8-9, 32
Homo sapiens 8-9
Homo sapiens neanderthalensis 4, 9, 18, 23, 32, 50
Homo sapiens sapiens 4, 8-9
horses 8-10, 16, 26-7, 30, 36, 46
hunter-gathering 4, 12, 14, 16, 21, 22-3, 38, 54, 60-61
hunting 26-7

I

Ice Age 5, 10
Inuit 24, 38-9, 47, 60

irrigation 7, 29, 56
ivory 15, 34-5, 42

J

Jericho 6, 51, 58
jewelry 40-41, 44
Jomon 54, 59

K

kayaks 46-7
knives 32, 34, 49

L

land bridges 6, 11
language 16-17
Lascaux caves 16
lighting 20-21
long houses 56

M

magic 41, 50-51
mammoths 5, 6, 10-11, 18-19, 26, 27, 36, 40
mastodons 5, 10-11
megaliths 52
Mesolithic 6, 12
metal-working 6-9, 46, 58, 60
migration 12-13, 26-7
music 15, 42

N

Native Americans 13, 14, 17, 19
Nazca people 37
Neanderthal people 4, 9, 18, 23, 32, 50
needles and pins 32, 34, 35, 38-9
Nenet people 39, 60
Neolithic 6, 19
Newgrange passage grave 9, 53
nomads 12-13

P

Palaeolithic 6
Papua New Guinea 15, 40, 60
passage graves 9, 52-5

pottery 5, 7, 14, 23, 36-7, 42-3, 50, 54, 57, 59

R

radiocarbon dating 4
reindeer 10-12, 25, 26, 34, 39
religion 14, 50-55
rhinoceroses, woolly 6, 10, 11, 36
rock art 5, 7, 15, 31, 34, 42, 46, 48, 49, 50

S

sculptures 5, 14, 15, 26-7, 36, 37, 42-3, 50, 54, 58-9
shamanism 14, 50-51
sheep 6, 7, 9, 13, 30-31, 38
shelter 18-19
sickles 28, 34
Skara Brae 9, 19, 20, 38, 40
social structure 14-15
spears 26, 32-3, 34, 49
spear-throwers 26, 32, 34-5
stone 4, 19, 28, 32-3, 37, 42, 44-5, 48, 61
stone circles 9, 52-3
Stonehenge 9, 52-3

T

tools 4, 5, 6, 9, 20-21, 22, 24-5, 26, 28, 32-5, 44-5
towns and cities 6, 8, 57-9
trade 13, 16, 44-5, 58-9
transport 7, 8, 46-7
tundra 11, 13, 26, 27

V

Venus figurines 5, 14, 36, 42, 50
villages 28-9, 56-7

W

warfare and weapons 33, 48-9
weaving 13, 36-8
wheel 8, 46
wood 4, 34-5, 48
wool 36, 38
writing 9, 16-17